"...I am so proud that I know you. This book is powerful and such a legacy for your family to have their miracle story in print... An inspiring depiction of love and faith. It is truly a must-read for all book clubs..."

Dr. Paula W. Adams
Sam Houston University Professor

"...[Mr. Martin's] writing puts me in a mental movie.... My skin still itches from the mosquitoes, and my mind is still trying to wrap around the power of the forgiveness...."

Carl Goshy, Home Builder, Trumpeter

"...Very powerful....a wonderful history of...family.... God does work in mysterious ways."

Edith Rutledge

"...I enjoyed *Welford Street Miracles* so much, I even had a few tears. Praise the Lord!!!

I am so fortunate to have met you, Richard. I will have to tell you how you and the Lord have blessed me."

Virgil Jorgensen

"...You represent [the west side of Port Arthur] well.... Thank you!"

Professor Donald P. Linden, M. Ed
Houston Community College District

"…Like going back in time. …A young man away from home with life's trials and tribulations, making the ultimate sacrifice to hopefully provide for [his] family in [his] absent as [his] parents…provided for [him] in [his] youth….I believe in miracles."

Pauline Brown-Linden

WELFORD STREET

Miracles

To Marolyn

Be Prepared to Witness

Miracles from the Westside

Be Blessed

WELFORD STREET

Miracles

A STRANGER'S TOUCH,
A LIFE RESTORED

R. MERIAL MARTIN

TATE PUBLISHING & *Enterprises*

Published by Tate Publishing & Enterprises, LLC
127 E. Trade Center Terrace | Mustang, Oklahoma 73064 USA
1.888.361.9473 | www.tatepublishing.com

Tate Publishing is committed to excellence in the publishing industry. The company reflects the philosophy established by the founders, based on Psalm 68:11,
"The Lord gave the word and great was the company of those who published it."

Book design copyright © 2009 by Tate Publishing, LLC. All rights reserved.
Cover design by Kellie Southerland
Interior design by Blake Brasor

Published in the United States of America

ISBN: 978-1-60696-049-3
1. Biography & Autobiography / Personal Memoirs
2. Religion / Inspirational
09.03.24

Author's Note

Out of respect for their privacy, I have changed the names of some of the people whose names appear in these pages.

Dedication

Welford Street Miracles is dedicated to my parents, Moses and Ida Martin, formerly of 1136 Welford Avenue, Port Arthur, Texas, and currently residing in heaven.

Anyone who met them liked them. They were "for real," never neglecting their duties at home but always finding time for others. There were nieces and nephews they cared for, along with the help of their other sisters. There were grandchildren they raised to help parents get through college or get their lives together. There were neighbors' children and children whose parents were friends of one of their children. It became a reason to live and seek good health in order that they could still support their grandchildren. "Children around the house keeps us young," they would often say.

Everyone in our extended family of the Mitchells and Martins know traits like this were evident in all their sisters and brothers. They all reached out to help family and others, a trait they expressed that they wanted their children to continue. Their wishes for their children included not closing their lives in a selfish way, but rather opening their lives to experience more of family and to help those willing to help themselves.

Ida loved to read, loved to talk, loved to eat, and it was when her health began to fail and she still wanted to do these things, but could not, that everyone knew her life on this earth was short. She did not like being helped. She did not like being a burden. She rejected help because she was the helper. She was the shepherd of the flock. She was the rock of Gibraltar in our family. She managed the meager finances, so we never wanted for any essentials. She was able to support us in school activities, so we were never left out. She managed to help some of us through college and others with help in their marriages.

Many people talk today about how much they have to do and actually wind up doing very little. Ida and Moses talked little and did much. Their years, like his gardens, were well kept, neat, and pretty. Many people cannot make time to raise one child. They raised eight children, many grandchildren, and helped to raise many other children.

Moses and Ida certainly did not live a pain-free life. They knew personal suffering. From her arthritis to the physical ravages of diabetes and his constant back pain and diabetes, they were well acquainted with trauma and anguish. Their faith and fortitude were always constant faces peering at the people around them through their personal clouds. They knew how to live graciously in a messy world.

They were parents with a commitment to helping others get through life, parents who never gave up on family, parents who hurt inside when their help was not used wisely or received in an understanding spirit, but they never stopped giving.

Although our parents' physical presence has gone from us, their spirit and influence have not. Someone will always be here who will remember Daddy and Mother. They remain in the recesses of our hearts, minds, and souls.

Ida and Moses knew God. What remains for us to do for them is to place in our own children and grand-children the same deposit of love and hope, determina-tion and vision, and the thirst for excellence that these God-fearing parents placed in us. It is my prayer that this story in print will accomplish that goal.

We all experience loss at some time. When someone loved is no longer with us, Jesus helps us fill those voids. He helps us focus again on the fact that all those who have gone before us are in the better place. Jesus will help us again.

Many have heard the *Miracle of Welford Street*. Mother told us that story many years ago. The Word of God opened their eyes when they learned they should be helpful to strangers.

We know God told them, "You were good and faith-ful shepherds of my many needy. You have done well. I have prepared a place for you."

Ida and Moses, this is your story as well as mine. It is a lesson for all the family members, friends, and strang-ers who were touched by your sharing and giving.

Acknowledgment

I want to acknowledge the inspiration given me by Hollywood writer Harry Essex. This former New Yorker wrote, co-wrote, or directed dozens of movies and numerous TV shows during his lengthy Hollywood career. I met him in 1984 when his small yacht was moored in Marina Del Rey next to my wife's grandparents, the Schmolls' large sailboat. He reviewed several manuscripts that I had written. He gave me a handwritten review of my works. I treasure his notes and keep them in a safe place. He loved the true stories of Welford Street. He encouraged me to pursue it to the fullest and add a central character whose life was influenced by Welford Street Miracles. It took time for the life of that main character to develop beyond what was fact in 1984. Harry, I pray that you are reviewing me from above.

Foreword

Welford Street Miracles is based on something you know something about. Something you experienced through the sense of life, of actual living, and that always makes for the best kind of writing. Its simplicity, its honesty in telling is evident not only in the lines but *between* the lines, and that's when writing is at its best. You believe the miracle, and believing it you begin to see the characters and feel for them and hope for them spiritually. Into this group of people we have a main character. Your prime subject wrought with a medical problem, brainwashed in his spiritual hierarchy, and skilled in the business world, whose struggles and accomplishments come to the forefront and whose encounter with a stranger ends in the greatest miracle of all. The best of everything as you advance your writing career.

Harry Essex, writer, producer-director

Introduction

Based on a true story, this novel is written to describe all the families on Welford Street who were instrumental in the development of the main character and all the Martin children. I also wanted to describe the early days and the early history of Port Arthur, Texas, and especially the west-side neighbors. I want to acknowledge the families who had their own miracles.

I want readers to *be* there during the times and during the miracles. The background is necessary to lead into the story of the main character, Richard, and his miraculous journey that commences in Port Arthur on Welford Street. This in itself is a fast-paced story of the business accomplishments, medical setbacks, and trials Richard faces as he strives to establish a spiritual and financial legacy for his family.

Welford Street
Miracles

Port Arthur is on State Highway 87 on the lower west bank of Sabine Lake, five miles east of the Neches River Rainbow Bridge and seventeen miles southeast of Beaumont in southeast Jefferson County, Texas. It was founded by Arthur E. Stilwell, a Kansas railroad promoter, who, in 1894, launched the Kansas City, Pittsburg, and Gulf Railroad. His intention was to link Kansas City to the Gulf of Mexico, and, originally, the Gulf Coast terminus was to be Sabine Pass. However, Stilwell changed his mind, evidently because he could not reach an acceptable agreement with Luther and Herman Kountze, New York bankers who owned most of the land around Sabine Pass. By December 1895, Stilwell and his backers had acquired land on the western shore of Sabine Lake and begun platting a city, which the promoter named for himself and which became a municipality in 1895. Stilwell envisioned Port Arthur as a major tourist resort as well as an important seaport; proximity to the lake and a mild climate convinced him that visitors could be easily attracted to the area. In his attempt to transform this marshy terrain into a tropical garden, Stilwell never lost sight of his primary endeavor, which was to make it a port city. In June 1896, the Port Arthur Channel and Dock Company was established, and in April 1897, it began cutting a canal along the western edge of the lake to deep water at Sabine Pass. Legal hurdles thrown up by the Kountze brothers delayed the project, but Port Arthur finally became a port in fact as well as in name in March 1899. Meanwhile, the city showed signs of steady progress. By the fall of 1897, it had 860 residents, and the following spring it was incorporated. A mayor-council government was established, but it gave way to the commission system in 1911. A city manager-commission system was implemented in 1932.

Despite his achievements, Stilwell was replaced as Port Arthur's chief financial backer in the early twentieth century by John W. "Bet a Million" Gates, a noted Wall Street plunger. After the Kansas City, Pacific, and Gulf went into receivership in the spring of 1899, Stilwell's role in Port Arthur ebbed quickly and ended in January 1904. Gates arrived in Port Arthur in December 1899 and was in the city periodically thereafter until his death in August 1911. His major concerns, like Stilwell's, were the port and canal. Port Arthur became an official port of entry in 1906, and by 1908, the Sabine-Neches Canal had been deepened and extended up the Neches River to Beaumont and Orange. Extension of the canal was a mixed blessing, though, because it cut Port Arthur off from Sabine Lake and thereby diminished the city's prospects as a tourist resort. Aside from business, Gates' legacy included Port Arthur College, a business and radio school founded in 1909, and Gates Memorial Library, funded by Mrs. Gates in 1918 as a memorial to her husband and son.

Stilwell and Gates may have started the city, but the eruption of Spindletop on January 10, 1901, secured its future. The Jefferson County Spindletop oil discovery was the largest crude oil find in the world to date. Major oil companies—Gulf, Magnolia, Humble, and Texaco— all emerged from the Spindletop oilfield boom. Gulf (in 1901) and Texaco (in 1902) started building major refineries at Port Arthur. Pipelines tied the city to Spindletop, and petroleum products soon were shipped through the canal. By 1909, Port Arthur had become the twelfth largest port in the United States in value of exports, and by 1914, it was the second largest oil-refining point in the nation. Development as a major petrochemical center was reflected in population growth. From nine hundred residents in 1900, Port Arthur expanded to a population of 7,663 in 1910 and 50,902 in 1930.

The 1929 crash and subsequent depression had not affected the residents of this small southeast Texas oil town that is surrounded by the four major refineries. The thriving shipping industry was instrumental in Port Arthur's becoming a port of entry in 1906. By 1947, Port Arthur was known as the center of the world's prosperous oil-refining facilities. "We oil the World" was its slogan. Notable citizens of Port Arthur have left their impact on the country: Mildred "Babe" Didrikson, Robert Rauschenberg, Alan Shivers, Jimmy Johnson, Janis Joplin, Evelyn Keyes, Buddy Benz, Mack H. Hannah, Jr., G. W. Bailey, Andrew Green, and many others. These notable citizens are honored in the wonderful Museum of the Gulf Coast in downtown Port Arthur.

The West Side

In 1938, nearly every male worked at a refinery or oil-related industry. Refining, pipelines, marine services, shipping, and shipbuilding were also major enterprises in this seaport town. Negroes were not allowed to live on the east side, but there were mulattos passing for white who were never revealed to their east-side neighbors. East side and west side were typically defined by the Southern Pacific railroad tracks that went north and south through the city. Negroes rarely crossed the tracks except to work in white businesses or white homes as domestics. In addition, they crossed the tracks to shop in the downtown stores that started at the railroad station and continued eastward; stores like The Fair, Bluesteins, Rexall Drug Store, S & H Kress Five and Dime, Western Auto, Holley-Andrews, and Plettman's Grocery. Negroes and whites kept to themselves in those days. At the refineries, Negroes, no matter how educated or skilled, were relegated and held down to jobs that were menial or jobs of hard labor.

The homes on Welford Street were wood frame and built on two-foot-high brick or concrete footings because the city is below sea level. The area would flood if there were heavy rainstorms or a hurricane. They were built on twenty-five-foot frontage by seventy-five-foot deep lots and had ten feet of clearance between each house. The homes were so close that wives could gossip through their kitchen windows while they cooked and performed their daily chores. They held conversations as if they were in the same room. Each house had a front porch and a screened-in back porch.

In the summertime, many refinery workers rode home for lunch on company horses or mules and were usually served lunch on their back porches. The homes were not built energy efficient in those days and were hot in the summer and cold in the winter. Fans were used for cooling. Potbelly stoves in the kitchens and wood-burning heaters in the living room heated the homes in the winter. Whites on the east side had natural gas heaters and could afford to have a floor furnace and swamp coolers. Eventually, Negroes would get natural gas for heating and cooking stoves. As soon as the white contractors ran out of east-side customers, they would begin their sales and installations on the west side.

There were hundreds of families on the west side, and everyone knew one another. Work, schools, and churches were the environments where they met. The neighborhoods were safe in those days because neighbors trusted each other like family. They knew who to trust and who to look out for. In the summertime, homes were unlocked, and at night windows and doors were opened to keep the houses cool. There were screens to keep the plague-like mosquitoes out. Residents would leave their houses open during the day and go to work or to church and never worry about intrusions or burglaries.

Moses and Ida Martin lived in this oil-rich refinery center of Port Arthur, Texas. Moses was born in Lafayette Parish, Louisiana, in 1910, and Ida in Youngsville, Louisiana, in 1918. He had the light brown-colored skin of his Indian and white heritage on his mother's side, and he had a French-African heritage on his father's side. He was a poor but strapping handsome Black man who, when he dressed up, had the dapper looks of a rich Negro. He always owned three name-brand suits, Stacy Adams and Florsheim shoes, Swede hats, and matching ties and hankies. Moses grew up on a Louisiana horse ranch and cotton farm with his six siblings.

His father, Valentine Martin, had come to Louisiana through the Port of New Orleans from France, where his parents had been African slaves. Valentine had been skilled in training horses. Many white horse owners paid him to train their Tennessee Walkers. He would teach the owners how to make the horses use their inherited gait. Valentine often explained that you cannot teach a horse this gait. He would teach the horses to perfect the gait. He also trained the horses to snap their teeth in time to the gait. The Tennessee Walkers' gaits were favored by country doctors who spent many hours on horseback; traveling preachers, who rode from church to church, practicing their sermons on the way, and preferred these fast and steady walking horses; as well as Louisiana property owners who used these easy riding horses to survey their immense land holdings and sugar cane fields.

Valentine also raced horses. He was a serious gambler who lost all of his land and horses playing poker.

Moses' mother, Rose, was half Native American and half-white Creole. Her researched lineage is tied to a son of the decorated Civil War General Jean Jacques Alexandre Alfred Mouton. The general's likeness is depicted in a statue in front of old city hall in downtown Lafayette, Louisiana.

His son, Jacques Dupre Mouton, is believed to have fathered Rose through her mother, who was a Native American slave. Many of Rose's cousins are white Moutons and live in Lafayette. She separated from Valentine and moved her children to Duson and then Lafayette after he had squandered away all their properties and sharecropper property rights. Moses, Suzette, and Alphonse, the oldest three children, dropped out of school to pick cotton and learn carpentry skills and mechanical trades on adjoining sharecropper farms to help their mother make ends meet. The youngest four, Lester, Oris, Alma, and Olivia, would concentrate on schooling and picking cotton, although Olivia could only watch her siblings work, as she was the baby and not old enough to work the fields.

Moses did not finish elementary school and could not read or write very well. Today, he might be defined as illiterate, but he was always able to cover up his shortcomings. He had a sense of the world and skills that would allow him to convince others that he understood even though he could not read. That made it easy for him to get a job at the Gulf Oil refinery, called "the

Gulf" by residents of Port Arthur, once he had ventured out on his own, moved to Port Arthur, and found work as a laborer in 1930.

Ida moved to Port Arthur in the mid-1920s with her siblings and her parents, Joseph and Elzina Mitchell. She was a brown-skinned woman with a figure that intrigued most young men. The family lived on Fifteenth Street on the west side, and Ida attended Lincoln School but did not graduate high school because she married Moses at age seventeen. She helped her husband understand signs, street names, store names, and traffic signs by sight. He could look at a sign or a building and say its name as though he were reading it. He had no problem with recognition. Later in their marriage, he would attend night school and learn to read, write, and sign his name. He was too proud to allow his children to teach him to read and write. His children would carry a lot of guilt about not using their knowledge to help him become more educated. There would be times when they would be embarrassed in front of their friends when it was clear that he could not read. Ida was busy being the homemaker and learning to cook, tend house, and take care of her husband and children.

After Ida's father died, her mother, Elzina, married Paul Brouchette. Ida had seven siblings. Ernestine married Merrill Williams and lived in Sabine Pass, Texas. Sabine Pass was only eight miles from Port Arthur. Nolia married Willie Honore and lived in Lake Charles, Louisiana. Andrew was a war veteran and career soldier who settled in Dallas after marrying Rose and retiring. Rosa Mae married Naulton Doffeny and died following the birth of her seventh child. Paul was also a career army soldier and married Ruth, a beauty from Los Angeles. They divorced, and Paul married a Korean woman and settled in Portland, Oregon, after retirement. Thomas spent a lot of years in the navy. He would have many marriages, none lasting as long as his final one with Shirley, a Korean woman. Tom's last stay was in Houston, where he died at an early age. Mary, the baby girl, would graduate from Sacred Heart High and marry Lloyd Hebert, who was reared in Ames, Texas. They would build a small house on the rear of their lot in the 700 block of Welford Street. Later, they would build a larger house in front of it and use the small one as a rental.

Moses and Ida were brought up in the Catholic Church. They attended Mass every Sunday at Sacred Heart and some weekday mornings when Moses was not on the day or graveyard shift. Their children would grow up as Catholics, learning to say their prayers in the morning and before bed and all during the day if they were attending the Catholic school. They would be faithful in following the religious rules of that time, which included eating fish every Friday, going to Confession every Saturday, never missing Mass on Sunday, and fasting during Lent every year. They would grow up believing in guardian angels and praying to saints. In 1936, Moses and Ida had their first son, Vincent.

Ida gave birth to seven children during the early years: Vincent, Rosita, Maurice, Richard, Barbara, Anthony, and Carl. Number seven, Carl, was born in 1949. Number eight, Althea, was born in 1957. Between seven and eight, Ida worked for two of the

doctors that her neighbor, Mrs. White, had worked
for previously. Ida did house cleaning and worked as a
maid. Sometimes Ida would go with the doctor's family to Galveston to work and live with them for two
weeks on the beach during their vacations. She also
worked at night cleaning the offices at the Standard
Brass Company but would be home before Moses, who
usually worked graveyard shifts, would leave for work.
However, it was in the evenings around 8 p.m. that the
houseful of kids would have to be quiet. That was when
Moses would go to bed before getting up around 11
p.m. to go to work.

It is hard to imagine, but two adults and seven children would live and sleep in a house that had a living
room with a couch-bed where Rosita and Barbara slept,
a dining room, a kitchen, and a master bedroom for
Moses, Ida, and the current baby. There was a bedroom
for Richard, Anthony, and Carl, the three youngest
boys, and the two oldest boys, Vincent and Maurice,
slept in a converted back porch that had a large bed
and only six inches clear on one side to walk or slide
their feet. Eventually, the square footage would grow
as Moses and his brother-in-law, Lloyd Hebert, would
add rooms to the rear of the house.

1100 Block Welford Neighbors

Emory and Louise White lived at 1100. Emory was tall, had a thin build, and worked at the Gulf refinery. Louise was a stout woman and worked as a housekeeper for wealthy doctors on the east side. Emory was very flexible and often showed the boys in the neighborhood how he could touch the top of his head with either foot and then with both at the same time.

They kept the most meticulous house on the block. Credit some of that to the fact that they had no children. They painted the interior and exterior every other year. It was through them that the Martin boys learned the skills of house painting. Mrs. White would teach the strokes of neat painting in the interior and Mr. White on the exterior wrought-iron railings on the front porch. Mr. White taught most of the boys how to cut grass and use one of the first power lawn mowers on the block. The Martins also learned how to keep the White's new cars clean and waxed.

The Whites bought a barbeque business and hired boys in the neighborhood. This is where the boys would learn to clean the place, cook food, stuff and smoke the famous juicy hot links, and wait tables. While they did not have children of their own, they did lay claim to Maurice and Richard Martin of 1136. Through their formative years, the Martin boys learned many skills from the Whites.

Many times, the Whites seriously asked Ida and Moses Martin to allow them to adopt the boys. The Martins' sons were well liked because the other neighbors, John and Elnora Beard at 1147, and Walter and Prova Zeno at 1148, wanted to adopt them as well.

Joseph and Jean Junius lived at 1108. Mr. Joe worked as a laborer at the Texas Company and on weekends as a baker at Mrs. Barnes' Cafeteria on the east side. Jean was a homemaker. They had one son, Joe, Jr., who always thought he was the toughest kid in the neighborhood. He did have the toughest German shepherd dog. All the boys on the block laid claim to Rex. Everyone fed him and everyone made him fight other block dogs. He would win every dogfight. Rex never killed an opponent but always made it cower, tuck tail, and run away.

Mr. Joe was an alcoholic, but that was not something people talked about then. At least Mr. Joe was able to control his problem, stay out of trouble, and keep working two jobs for most of his life. When the Martin boys were old enough, Mr. Joe would take a couple with him to work at the cafeteria. They would learn to use automated dishwashing machines and hand wash the large pots and pans. Sometimes they would stock shelves in the storeroom and deliver the large vegetable cans to the cooks. For their reward, they got to sample the most excellent pull-apart dinner rolls ever made and a piece of Mrs. Barnes' famous fried chicken. They never were allowed to go into the dining room when there were customers. Only whites worked up front. At the end of the day, everyone in the back partook of the food that did not sell. Every workday there was food to take home.

Everything in Port Arthur seemed big during those times. At that time, none of the children had been to the big cities like Los Angeles. However, once they experienced exposure to a crowded, big city and lots of other than southern Texas people who spoke proper English, everything in Port Arthur seemed small. For most of the Westside families, that travel experience would not come until they had graduated from high school and went off to college or the military.

Columbus Wilson was a muscular man with a manicured mustache and lived at 1112. He was a divorcee and lived alone. Well, not always alone. He was the adult playboy on the block. He would often bring his girlfriends home. Columbus seemed to always have a Cadillac or a Buick Roadmaster. He liked the big cars. When convertibles came out, he had to have one.

All the kids called him by his first name. It was unusual for that time, but Columbus approved. He liked the nightlife so well that he owned and ran a few beer halls and private clubs. He did this in addition to working at the Gulf. He had great carpentry skills and, after removing a large pecan tree, built a two-story rental at the back of his seventy-five-foot-deep lot. Pecan trees were in nearly all the backyards, and there were hedges in the front that served as a fence between properties. Upstairs there were two apartments with a kitchen, bedroom, and a bathroom each. On the bottom, he built a one-car garage to house his Roadmaster, and a one-room combo with a bathroom.

Columbus later built a two-story addition to the rear of 1112 after he got married to a woman who had a daughter by him.

Often, Columbus would pay the Martin boys to do odd jobs for him. From hauling lumber to actually nailing boards by following his instructions, the boys got to learn a lot about carpentry when he built or remodeled his rentals and the addition.

George and Joyce Martin lived at 1140. George worked at the Gulf, and Joyce was a homemaker who also did some domestic work on the east side. She was a good seamstress who made dresses and shirts out of flour sacks. Most of the women in the 1100 block bought flour and rice sacks with designer patterns. They would sew them into clothing or save them until they had enough to stitch a quilt.

They had a son and a daughter. However, before they were born, Mr. Green, Joyce's father, lived with them. He was retired, and his only mission was to play dominos and checkers and drink the best aromatic coffee around. You knew when Mr. Green was sitting on their back screened porch because you smelled his pipe tobacco and his Seaport dark roast blend coffee.

George was a good baseball player. He and his wife were fair skinned because of the Louisiana Mouton heritage. George and his brothers changed their name from Mouton to Martin when they moved to Texas. Martin was more of a Negro name than the many white Mouton relatives in Louisiana. The Moutons were cousins to Moses Martin through his mother, whose maiden name was Mouton.

George was a catcher on the Port Arthur Negro League team. They played almost every summer weekend in cities around southeast Texas and across the border into Louisiana. Their home games were at Lincoln High School field, which was one block from Welford Street. Hundreds of adults and kids in the neighborhoods would go to watch them play. There was never an admission price. The players were good role models for the high school players and often helped the baseball coach teach and train the team. There were very few home run souvenir balls because on the other side of the left field fence was the Texaco refinery yard. A large ditch that was filled with contaminated oil silt and water would swallow up most balls hit over the fence. One could see where the ball entered the crude, but no one wanted to slip under the fence to attempt retrieval. It was the same after high school games.

Joyce was a good cook and made her specialty every Saturday. She made the best lemon meringue pie. She always made enough to share with the neighborhood kids after they did minor chores for her. It seemed that she always had pie in her icebox. The iceman knew this and would always get his slice every other day on his delivery. Whites on the east side were getting rich on ice. Every house had to have a twenty-five or fifty-pound block every day or every other day. Cost: twenty-five or fifty cents. One west side Black man was killed right after he opened an icehouse and started selling cheaper than the whites. By the time Blacks opened icehouses again, electric refrigerators were in most of the homes.

Emile and Julia Prevost lived at 1146. They were an older couple that had some kids who were grown and married. Pie, a daughter, and Jr. Prevost lived in the house during those years. They were still older than most of the kids on the block.

Jr. Prevost played football at the high school, and Pie would graduate and go to college. She came back as a teacher and taught at the Sacred Heart Elementary School. Later she would marry and have her reception at 1146. This was the first wedding of children who lived on the block, and all neighbors were invited. The reception was held outside in the backyard. That was good news because Miss Julia used snuff and smoked a pipe. Their house reeked of snuff and pipe tobacco. Jr. smelled like snuff. Anyone who spent fifteen minutes in that house would smell like snuff.

Jr. Prevost taught all the boys on the block how to make kites from scratch. He would find some small straight branches for the frame, and he would use the funny papers from the *Sunday Port Arthur News*. He used flour and water to make the glue and old rag strips to make the tail. Then he would spend a day's wages that Mr. Branch would pay him for delivering newspapers to buy a ball of twine. Jr. was great at kite making. He also made "fighting kites." He would put some of his dad's old single-edge razor blades at the end of the frame and use them to cut the strings of other kids' kites. He was a great kite fighter and had a strategy of making his kite dance nearer another kite and would jerk his line so his would strike another kite line and cut it on an upward ascent. He was not a cruel kite fighter. He only did that maneuver if everyone had razor-edged kites too. Jr. Prevost was a good teacher and made other boys good kite fighters. It was not long before he, too, would become a kite runner (chasing his kite that lost the battle) and not always the last kite flying.

Walter and Prova (pronounced "proove-ah") Zeno lived at 1148. Mr. Walter worked at the grain docks at the shipyard. He walked to work a lot. Sometimes he would ride on a truck that went through the west side picking up and dropping off shift workers; however, only if he was bone tired and the truck was on time. After all, it was just eleven city blocks to his house. There was also a truck for the Gulf and one for the Texas Company. Most of the men on the block used the trucks.

Mr. Walter would come home looking like a ghost. He would be covered from head to toe in grain dust. The only skin one could see was around his nose and eyes where he had worn a mask to protect his lungs. Even with the mask, he should not have lived as long as he did. He always smelled like grain dust. Even when he was in a suit of clothes, and that was not too often, he smelled like chicken feed. Only a wedding or a funeral would cause him to rough it in a suit, as he would say.

Miss Prova was a godly and sweet old woman. Miss Prova loved to garden, and her flowerbeds were the talk of the west side. Only Mrs. Beard in the house across from her gave her competition on the block. Miss Prova lived longer than any woman on the block. She died at ninety-eight.

Mr. Walter was a vegetable gardener like Moses. They would share okra, melon, and tomato seeds. The best of Mr. Walter was that he was the superior hunter on the block and possibly on the west side. He raised hunting dogs. The predominant breed was Black 'N' Tan. Mr. Walter and Mr. Moses would go hunting often and bring back rabbit, big squirrels, raccoons, and duck. It was often said that the reason he was a good bird game hunter was the grain smell. Game was attracted to him. Mr. Walter taught Maurice and Richard of 1136 how to care for the dogs and how to hunt.

He always had good hunting stories to tell. Amongst hunters, it is the stories of the old timers that teach the art and skill of pursuing the game. You always listened to Mr. Walter. Mr. Moses and Maurice tell the story about the prize dog that did not listen to Mr. Walter. The dog, named Blue, was on the other side of an irrigation canal. Mr. Walter was done hunting and called Blue. Then he gave him his last chance to respond to hand signals. The dog did not listen, so Mr. Walter shot him.

On the other side of the street, at 1147, lived John and Elnora Beard. They did not have children of their own until 1960, after I had graduated from high school, when they adopted a son. Balding on the top, round, and chunky, Mr. John worked at the Gulf. He was a Prince Hall mason and achieved the highest rank of M.W. Grand Master in the Masonic group. He was well respected on the west side for spearheading the building of the new Masonic hall in the new addition.

He would often travel to conventions across the nation. He did not talk too much about his accomplishments, but he would show pictures of his travels to Richard Martin, the boy he wanted to adopt.

In fact, John Beard asked Moses and Ida so many times that Moses would jokingly accuse Ida of having John's son, Richard. "Why does he want him so much if that is not the case?" he would ask Ida.

In addition, he would tell me, over and again, the story of how the Prince Hall Masons had a proud and storied history, which was, in characteristic Mason fashion, extremely well documented.

In 1775, Prince Hall, a free Black man of East Indian extraction, along with fifteen other Black men, was inducted into a lodge in Boston. The lodge consisted primarily of members of the British Army who were stationed in Boston. These soldiers were attached to the British Army as part of the 38th Regiment of Foot and attached to the Grand Masonic Lodge as Lodge No. 441 Irish Constitution. The name given to these freemen's lodge after the departure of the British in 1776 was the African Lodge No. 1. The new society there established was one of as stringent moral value and exclusivity of character as any other white lodge of the day. Lodge 441, prior to departure, granted African Lodge No. 1 the right to meet and observe Masonic code under dispensation. Seeking full recognition as a viable and legitimate lodge, Prince Hall applied to the Grand Lodge of England itself on March 2, 1784. Mr. Hall was forced to resort to appealing to a foreign lodge for a charter in much the same way, as did the largely Semitic lodges in Germany. After repeated applications to domestic lodges, these freemen and Jews were forced by necessity to seek recognition from a higher and possibly more egalitarian Grand Lodge. The petition was granted on September 29, 1784. It was delivered to Boston on April 29, 1787, by James Scott, John Hancock's brother-in-law, and thus African Lodge No. 459.[1]

Miss Elnora was a homemaker. Her sister, Elzina "Blackie" Wagner, lived in the next block at 1038 and was my godmother. Like Miss Prova, Miss Elnora took care of the house and planted flowers. Most of the men on the block considered themselves the best angler. However, the best was really Miss Elnora. She fished during the week and weekends when Mr. John was traveling to a meeting or convention. She and Blackie would put those long cane poles and crabbing gear into her car and head off for the jetties. Sometimes they would fish at Keith Lake near Sabine Pass and often drive to High Island toward Galveston and fish in the area before where the ferry crosses the channel. She knew all the good fishing holes off the highways and country roads. Sometimes they would take me along. They taught me to fish with a pole and a bobber and to catch blue crabs with twine, beef neck bones, and a net. They would argue over who would get me when the Martins finally decided to give me up. I spent more time with the sisters during the summer than I spent at home. At Christmastime, I always had more presents than the other Martin children. On Christmas Day, I had to spend time at the Beards' and at my godparents' so they could experience Christmas and have a child in the house to open presents. Every December in Jefferson County, Church Charity groups would sponsor a party for children of families chosen by the participating churches. All of the Martin children would remember boarding a Southern Pacific train in Port Arthur about three days before Christmas. It took them to Beaumont, where they walked to a nearby auditorium for a Christmas party . The income of the Martin family, and most families on the west side, qualified to be included in the party. They would all receive gifts to take back home and place under the Christmas tree.

Paul and Mary Payton lived at 1025. Miss Mary was a Creole (a person born in Louisiana but of usually French ancestry) and she had a rent house on her property. Ida Martin's mother lived in the rent house for a few years until she died. Miss Mary was the first in the neighborhood to have a TV. Every weekday at 4 p.m., all the Martin kids would go there to watch *Howdy Doody*.

Miss Mary and Ida Martin would talk over the phone every morning. They kept up with their Creole language by doing so. At 1024, across from Miss Mary, lived Cousin Eran. Eran was a Mouton and was cousin to Moses Martin and George Martin of 1140. Before Moses owned a car, Eran did, and she would drive the Martin clan all the way to Lafayette, Louisiana, to visit Moses' mother, Grandma Rose. That car was loaded with six or seven kids and three adults. Eran also carried a pot to pee in. There were stations along the way, but most did not have restrooms for colored people. Kids were stacked on laps, and occasionally someone would wet themselves and the lap underneath. All the kids in the neighborhood and in the school classrooms were immune to that pissy smell. Most of the elementary-age kids had that smell from wetting the bed or sleeping with a sibling who wet the bed and them too.

Eran would go to visit the Moutons while she was in Lafayette. They would stay a day or two and then she would drive them back to Port Arthur. However, while they were there, they would meet all their Mulatto, Caucasian, and "passing for white" cousins. Grandma Rose's house was filled with the smell of baked goods and sweet spices. She and her daughter, Alma (Aunt "Tee-Ma"), would bake teacakes and sweet fruit pies, and if there was a live pig, there would be fresh pork, boudain, and blood sausage made.

On one trip, Grandma Rose walked into the backyard where she had a young pig tied to the large fig tree. She had a large cooking pot in one hand and a knife in the other. She was talking to everyone about life, and no one knew what she was about to do. Before they knew what had happened, Grandma Rose tied the rear legs of the suckling, hoisted it up, and tied the rope to the large fig tree. With the pig hanging head down, she slit the pig's jugular, placed the pot under its neck, and drained its blood into the pot. Then the adults skinned and butchered the pig, and you would have to search for what was discarded. Even the hooves would get ground up into a medicinal powder. She used every part of that pig to make something edible or medicinal. Neighbors would come every Saturday to buy the sweet potato, yam, fig pies, and teacakes that she and Aunt Tee-Ma made.

The Martin clan would also visit their uncle Oris and aunt Adell. She was a schoolteacher, and he worked as a conductor for a railroad. It was a rare sight to see a Black conductor. He also had a dry cleaning business on Breaux Bridge Highway. Oris was best known for his days in the army as a French interpreter for General Patton in his contacts with DeGaulle. Everyone had to listen to Oris tell stories about DeGaulle's daughter and how she fell for him. Oris learned French from his father, Valentine, who rarely spoke Creole, although he knew it. Uncle Oris always said that his father did it to piss people off and make himself stand out. Whenever his father played cards or got angry, the French would predominate in his mixed speech.

There were many other families, relatives, and friendly neighbors in the seven, eight, nine, and ten hundred blocks that had impact on those who lived in the 1100 block, including Ida Martin's baby sister, Mary, who lived in the 700 block. She was married to Lloyd Hebert. He had served in the army and had one of the better labor jobs at the refinery because of his education and military experience.

Moses and Lloyd helped each other build additions onto their houses. They were excellent carpenters. As their families grew and there was a need, they would build another room.

West Side Uptown

It suffices to say that most blocks on the west side could compare to the 1100 block on Welford in types of families, identical characters, problems, successes, and pride of ownership. Each block would have their godly ones, alcoholics, hunters, carpenters, playboys, large families in cramped quarters, and possibly their own secret stories of religious phenomenon.

The red light district was the only area that was different. Seventh and Eighth Streets from Grannis Avenue to the railroad tracks were the blocks that most west side residents were repulsed by and stayed away from. Whites from the east side and merchant seamen from all over the world would frequent the whorehouses, gambling joints, beer halls, and nightclubs. Merchant seamen could be seen walking from the docks on the most western end of the city, where their ships were tied up, eastward down Seventh Street toward Grannis Avenue, or they would pile up in a Jack's or Comeaux's Taxis and head that way. Dutch Dibbles was the whitest-looking Negro on the west side. Dutch ran many of the red light businesses on Eighth Street. Eventually, the Southern Baptists would get the Texas State government and, specifically, an official who everyone remembers as "Mr. James" to shut down Eighth Street and send Dutch Dibbles and other owners underground to continue their activities. Prostitutes went from constant "John traffic" in the buildings to slow traffic on the Seventh Street corners near the booze joints. They did not have to worry about being arrested, because the city only hired two Negro police officers, and they spent most of their time policing the beer halls and making arrests of drunks. In the forties and early fifties, there was a stabbing or shooting most every weekday night and multiple deaths on the weekend. This was indeed the only different area on the west side, for the majority were just like the 1100 block of Welford.

Mack Hannah and Moody Funeral Homes did a bang-up business on the west side, and they both got rich. The booze- and crime-related deaths were a big boom, but the main contributor was the deaths because of the contamination from the refineries, which no employee or citizen in his right mind would complain about. The city leaders did not. Neither doctors nor the hospitals complained. There were more than what could be considered normal: miscarriages, birth defects, and all types of cancers, tumors, and early, unexplained deaths of men who worked at the plants. It seems like there were more than what should be considered normal for a city with a population of fifty thousand.

Visitors

The Martins rented various houses on the west side and, in 1936, rented the house at 1100 Welford. They rented a second house next door and then a third house next to that one, and they finally purchased the fourth house built on that block, 1136 Welford. It was while they were living in the third house at 1112 when a stranger came by for a visit.

It was August of 1937, and Ida was two months pregnant with their daughter, Rosita, who would be born in May of 1938. Moses rode home on one of the horses from work. The refinery gates were only six blocks from Welford Avenue.

And on this summer day, Ida was setting the small table on the back porch. Moses was always on time. Moses rode the big buckskin horse at a gallop down the dirt streets that were prevalent on the west side. The Saint Augustine grass was lush and green throughout the west side thanks to a hurricane two weeks prior and the resulting flood that covered the lawns for three days.

The east side had sewers to drain the rainwater and gravel or paved streets for their automobiles. The west side had oyster shell streets and ditches that drained toward the refinery canals. The streets were frequented by fruit trucks selling watermelons and vegetables, and large open-cab garbage trucks that smelled up the already funky air from the refineries. These large vehicles would crush the shells and make the streets easy for kids to walk barefoot on. Just about every day the Gulf refinery raised her dress and let everyone hear her whistles and smell her farts. Often one could hear that saying, "the Gulf raised her dress today" all over the city. It was the most offensive smell but not one that was publicly complained about. Only a few Negroes owned a used car in those days. It was not until the midfifties that almost every refinery worker on the west side would own a used car or brand new models.

Moses saw what appeared to be a white man walking in his direction in the 1000 block as he turned off 11th Street north onto his block, and he slowed the horse to a walk, making a crunching sound on each step on the oyster shell road. He turned his body in the saddle and looked back to determine if he recognized the man. *Maybe he is mulatto from Louisiana,* he thought. Many families looked white on the west side. He made the horse jump the ditch between the street and his yard, then walked the horse onto his front yard, stepped off, and tied the reins to a post on the front porch. At this point, he could no longer see the man because his visibility was blocked by fir trees and hedges in the front yard at 1108.

Ida, in her flour sack smock, met him at the front screened door and embraced him.

"I have a good lunch for you, Moses."

"Good, because they worked me hard this morning and I'm hungry."

"Well, as usual, I made plenty."

They walked through the living room that is sparsely furnished with a couch bed and a radio on a coffee table in the corner. There were black-and-white family pictures in small frames on the walls that were covered with flowery designs on the wallpaper. The dining room had a table and chairs and a hutch that housed a set of dishes that Ida ordered from the *Spiegel* catalog when they got married. Then they walked through the dining room and into the kitchen, where Moses washed his hands. He did not take off his dusty boots.

The kitchen had a metal cabinet with some drawers for storage and a sink. There was a gas stove with four small burners and an oven. For refrigeration, there was a Servel icebox to keep three days of food cool.

Ida went to the stove, picked up the prepared plate, walked onto the back porch, and set it on the table. She always served each meal on the good china plates. Moses is seated. He felt the cool breeze through the screened walls. The open field beyond his backyard was empty. Houses had not been built on the street behind their home. Beyond Roosevelt Street were the baseball, track, and football fields of Lincoln school. The field extended for four blocks. When there was a breeze, the back porch was the place to be.

"I think I saw a white man down the street. He was walking."

White people were rarely seen on the west side. Just three weeks ago, a white man had been caught by residents after he had attempted to rape a mulatto girl whose family lived on DeWalt Street, just three blocks from Welford. The police had come and taken him away before the mob could hurt him. No white man in his right mind would be caught this deep into the west side this soon.

Ida had warmed up beef stew with carrots and celery over rice. She had seconds in case Moses wanted more. When he went back to work, she would eat whatever warmed food was left. "Waste not, want not", she would eventually tell her children. Along with having eight children, that attitude would help her to eventually change her figure from fine to stout.

Moses began to eat while stirring the meat and gravy with the rice as Ida sat nearby. They heard a knock at the front door. Moses motioned with his hand for her to see who was there. Ida went through the kitchen and into the dining room. The wooden front door was open, but the screen door was shut. As she walked toward the door, she saw the outline of a white man with his back to the screen.

His hair was below shoulder length and was shaped meticulously. He was wearing brand-new blue overalls. His shirt was a beige starched tunic with three-quarter-length sleeves. It reminded her of the cachet and surplice worn by priest and altar boys at church. As she reached the screen door, he turned to face her and she saw that he had a bearded face and it too was meticulously groomed. His greenish eyes sparkle. Cautiously, Ida asked, "Yes, sir, what can I do for you?"

The stranger replied, "Ma'am, I'm hungry and I thought you might have a bite to eat to give me".

Ida stared at the stranger. Surely he could not be a beggar. Surely not in new overalls and such a nice shirt. Bare feet? The man was barefoot, she notices.

"I don't know. I'll have to ask my husband. Moses!" she yelled.

Hearing the loud call of his name, Moses ran through the house to her side.

"Who is this man and what does he want?"

Ida is speechless as she looked back and forth at Moses and at the stranger.

"Moses, he is hungry and needs something to eat."

Moses looked at Ida. She nodded her head affirmatively.

Their hospitality would never allow them to turn away any neighbor or visitor from food, especially a hungry one. That was the way of people in Louisiana and those who migrated to Port Arthur. Everywhere you go and knock on a door; residents would ask questions to determine if they knew someone you were kin to. Then, once they made a connection, they would not let you leave until you had something to eat. You could not refuse. Then you had to wait until they heated up some leftovers. Imagine that you were lost and looking for a family member's address and knocked on many doors; you could add twenty pounds before you found the family member's house. Then you would have to eat again.

"Well, okay, we have enough food. We can spare some, so come on in. Ida will fix you a plate."

Moses opened the screen door, and the stranger

walked into the living room and followed Ida. Moses noticed the way this man was dressed and his flowing, effortless style of walking. He also noticed that the bottoms of his bare feet were clean, and they left no dust tracks from the dirt and gravel road on the shiny varnished wood floor in the living and dining rooms. He could see his own dusty boot prints where he had walked earlier. However, the dust tracks never concerned him because Ida would always run the dust mop as soon as he went back to work.

Moses and the stranger are seated at the table on the cool back porch.

"What are you doing walking on the west side? Don't you know this is not a good time for a white man to walk on this side of town?"

"I have no knowledge of that being a problem. I only know that I am hungry and I am thankful for your hospitality."

Ida brought in food on the good china plate and set it down in front of the stranger.

"It's not much. We are poor people," Ida says.

He took several bites while *oohing* and *aahing* and said, "Poor? Ida and Moses, you are richer in more ways than the richest of men. You have taken me in and you don't know me but are helping to cure my hunger."

How did he know their names? Ida had called out Moses' name, and Moses did say Ida's name, but they did not recall that until later and now wondered how he heard and remembered. She looked at the hands and arms coming out of the tunic shirt. His hands were long with slender, manicured fingers. *They are beautiful,* she thought as she looked at her own. Her hands were not bad, considering she frequently dipped them into lye soap water to wash clothes, but she would not call them beautiful.

Finishing his lunch, Moses looked in Ida's direction.

"I've got to get back to work. Ida, make him a sack lunch to take with him."

"No, thank you. I'm traveling light."

Ida went into the kitchen anyway.

"Moses and Ida." He addressed them again and they both turned to listen.

"I tell you, you will never be without food or shelter, and you will always be good providers for your many children."

They did not reply. Yet, as Moses shook the hand of the stranger, he felt a twinge or sort of electrical shock in that handshake.

"You don't have to make a big thing out of this. Ida will still make you a sack. I've got to go back to work."

Moses, with his gold tooth sparkling, walked through the kitchen, tapped Ida on the head lovingly, and went toward the front door. Ida, with brown bag in hand, looked in the direction of the porch and saw the stranger, who had already gone outside through the back porch door, through the porch screen, walking toward the front between houses. Moses was out front near the horse. She ran to the front door.

"Moses, did you see him? He left and was walking toward the front yard."

"No, but I'll look on the side of the house."

Moses walked over between houses and saw no one. He bent to his knees and looked underneath the two houses. Because they were on brick pillars, one could crawl underneath. Seeing no one, he ran to the backyard and looked around. *If the man is on this block, I would be able to see him,* he thought. There were no houses on the back half of the block, and the open schoolyard extended for blocks. The stranger was nowhere in sight. Moses ran to the front yard. Ida was now holding the reins of the horse. Instinctively, he mounted the horse and galloped up and down the streets as Ida watched from the dirt road. Moses returned.

"I don't see him anywhere."

He saw a few other neighbors in their front yards as if they are looking for something. *They cannot be looking for that stranger,* he thought. *I had better not ask them. They would think something is wrong with me.*

He told Ida, "It is like he disappeared. Let's check the house again and let's not tell anybody about this."

They both went through the bedrooms and checked closets, even under the beds. Ida noticed Vincent is sound asleep and safe. She locked the doors in case the stranger came back. Moses promised to hurry back from work.

"I'll clean that up when I get home," he says, pointing to the fresh manure pile as he galloped off.

At 1140 Welford, Joyce had been having doubts about her popular baseball player husband, George, being faithful. George had told her that he would come home for lunch that day. She had also prepared lunch. She had been having problems getting pregnant and having a child, which she thought would make her marriage better. Her father, Mr. Green, was sitting on the back porch, smoking his pipe.

The stranger appeared at the back porch door and asked Mr. Green if he would like to play a game of checkers. The checkerboard was next to him on a small table that he had crafted. He loved to have an old friend come over, and they would play checkers or dominos for hours. Before he could realize that he had agreed to play with a stranger whom he had never seen before, they were playing a game.

Joyce heard the loud talking of her father and someone else. She thought that he and one of his old friends were playing games. She walked through the kitchen toward the porch, saying, "Papa, it looks like George is not coming for lunch again."

As she entered the doorway to the porch, she saw the stranger playing checkers with her father.

"Papa, who's this man,?" she asked.

Joyce looked at the meticulously dressed stranger with long, flowing hair and a manicured beard wearing a tunic with gold trimmings. Under the table, she could see that he was barefoot.

"This is my friend."

Mr. Green had been losing it in the last months. He had started forgetting and misplacing things.

Joyce thought he was having one of his moments. She knew the stranger should not be there. Before she could ask him to get out of her house, he spoke.

"George will be here soon. You can get his lunch ready."

"What? You know George too?"

Within seconds, she heard the front door open, and there was George.

"Where have you been? You're late for lunch again. Did you stop over at your girlfriend's?" she chastised George.

George walked into the kitchen and said, "There you go again with all that bullcrap about a girlfriend. Just give me my food!"

The stranger walked into the kitchen and stood between them.

George was at odds on what to say or do. His mind flashed back to his stop by his girlfriend's house to get a few hugs and kisses before continuing home for lunch. He thought about all the times and the different women with whom he had been unfaithful to Joyce. The pressure of the situation forced him to take a seat and blurt out, "Joyce, I am sorry. None of that will ever happen again."

George put both hands on his head and buried it in his lap and mumbled, "What am I saying? Why am I saying this?"

The stranger put a hand on the shoulder of George and the other hand on Joyce's back and said, "God forgives you and will give you a family that will draw you closer to each other."

Then he walked over to Mr. Green and touched him on the head, as Mr. Green stayed focused on the next checker move.

"You win, my friend. I will see you soon."

The stranger walked off the screened porch and between houses toward the front. George got up and ran to the front door, hoping to catch up with the stranger when he made it to the front yard. He looked in the yard and down the street but did not see him. George walked to the side of the house and looked between but did not see him. He looked to the south next door and two doors down and saw Moses and

Joe Junius from 1108 out in the front yard looking for something. He looked to the north and saw Miss Prova. In that moment, he did not realize that they could also be looking for the stranger.

He and Joyce never talked to anyone about the stranger until years later. There were days right after the visit when they had company over and Mr. Green told stories about the stranger and how he had played checkers with him. However, Joyce would immediately dismiss it as old age setting in.

George and Joyce began to share their life. George took her on baseball road trips. No longer would he go alone and give in to the temptations of the young women who followed the ballplayers from city to city.

Mr. Green died not long after the stranger's visit. "I will see you soon," the stranger had said. Ten years later, Joyce and George would start a family and have a boy and a girl.

Mr. Joe Junius, who lived in 1108 and was one of a handful who owned a 1935 Ford coupe, was driving his car in the 800 block on Welford Street when he swerved the car into a ditch on the side of the road to avoid hitting the stranger. Mr. Joe had finished off his daily pint. He always carried a pint of gin in his car. After getting off for lunch at the Texas Company, he had pulled over on the side of the road near the reservoir to finish off a pint.

He and Miss Jean had been arguing the night before about his alcoholism. It was a night like many nights in the past. They were always arguing about his drinking. She was a gypsy-looking woman because of the way she dressed and styled her long black hair. He was a short man who wore a mustache and was never without a fedora.

It was a sobering experience as he backed his car out of the ditch. He rolled the window down and asked the stranger if he was all right. He offered to drive the stranger to the east side, where he thought this white man was headed. *Why was he walking on the west side? And he was barefoot, but his feet were clean and not covered with the dust from the dirt and gravel streets.*

"After scaring you, come on, get in, and I'll take you out of here!"

Shouted Joe over the loud engine noise. The stranger accepted his offer and got into the passenger side of the car.

Driving across the railroad tracks toward the east side, Joe was as alert as if he had just started the day void of the effects of alcohol.

The stranger spoke up and asked, "Joe, have you figured out why you feel like you have not had a drink today?"

He thought *how does he know my name?* Suddenly, the arguments with Jean and the habit of stopping at his favorite liquor store twice a day flashed before him. He realized why drinking is bad for him and his family.

"Because I almost ran over you? How do you know my name and that I had a drink?"

"Well, your name is on your cafeteria work shirt hanging in the back by the window, and I see the empty gin bottle on the floorboard. Joe, drinking is not what God has in his plans for you. You must stop drinking before you ruin your marriage and influence the life of your son."

"What son?" Joe asks. "I don't have a son!"

"You will have a son in the next year. You must stop drinking for Jean to be with child."

Joe could not believe what he was hearing. He did not think about how the stranger knew his wife's name until he talked about the encounter days later. Could this be another dream? A dream like the ones he has so often when he has finished his daily pint.

Joe pulled over in front of a liquor store.

"This can't be happening to me. You just wait here until I come back from getting a pint."

Joe was walking back to the car and started to feel the effects of a drunken stupor. He barely made it to the car, tripped over a rock, and fell to the ground as the bottle broke and cut his hand. The stranger stepped out of the car and moved to his side, ripped off a sleeve from his tunic, and wrapped it around Joe's hand. He helped Joe into the passenger seat, placed his bare foot on the foot knob to start the engine, and drove the car back toward Joe's house.

"You need to turn around and take me to Dr. Gibson's office."

The stranger did not answer. He looked at the bloodied bandage and said,

"Joe, all will be well with you and your wife."

He pulled the car into Joe's front yard, where he parked on a gravel runway. The stranger gave Joe the keys, stood outside the car, and told him, "Joe, go inside. Jean is waiting for you. And remember, all will be well with you."

Joe walked to the locked front screened door and began banging on it. He looked back, but the stranger was not in sight. He called to Jean, who was on her way to the front door. He asks her, "Did you see that man?"

"What man?" Jean responded. She stepped on the porch and only saw Moses on a horse, George, and Miss Prova in their front yards. They all appeared to be looking for something or someone.

"Why do you have that cloth on your hand?"

Joe looked, and there was no blood on the sleeve from the tunic. In shock, he moved quickly into the house. He sat down and told Jean about the stranger.

"And he said that when I stop drinking, we will have a son."

Joe, Jr. was born one year after Joe gave up his bad habit. Jean wrapped the tunic sleeve around the crucifix on the living room wall. They would not repeat the story until years later. For years, the sleeve was there.

When Joe, Jr. was eight, his young aunt came to visit from California. Delores was ten years old. She stayed with them and went to school in Port Arthur. One day, Delores was cleaning house and she removed the sleeve from the crucifix. She thought it to be a cleaning rag left there during dusting. She had never been told the story about the stranger. She threw it into the trash barrel, and no one could find it.

The day after Joe, Sr. learned about the missing sleeve, he started drinking again. This time, he never gave up the habit. However, he was more moderate in his drinking. He always blamed it on the missing sleeve and the untimely strike at the Texaco refinery that caused them financial problems. He could always fall back on his weekend job as a baker and cook for Mrs.

Barnes' Cafeteria. Since he worked at the cafeteria on Sundays, he never had a link to a church.

By this time many of the neighbors assumed that Jean had gone to drinking also because she more or less became a hermit. She rarely came outside. Oh, you could see her in the backyard hanging clothing on the clotheslines. That was the only time. She used to visit Ida Martin all the time. Now Ida had to visit her, but that got old and was too one-sided.

On the day of the strange visits, Prova Zeno at 1148 was working in the flowerbed on the north side of her house. The plants had all been damaged during the hurricane two weeks ago. The refinery canal that was only fifteen feet from her house flooded, and all the oil contamination and silt had rose to the top and covered her plants. She always had the best flower garden on Welford. Now the plants were dying.

She was in tears when the stranger approached from the street. The 1100 block of Welford dead-ended at the refinery canal.

Miss Prova was busy working to clean the large zinnia stems by wiping them with old wet towels.

"You have an abundance of good plants in the front and on the south side. Why don't you transplant some of the good plants on this side and remove all these soiled ones?" asked the stranger.

Miss Prova did not have her glasses on. They were hanging on a string around her neck. When she wanted to see something up close, she would put them on. She looked in the direction of the stranger and did not notice too much about him. She assumed he was someone from the neighborhood.

"Who's that?" she asked. "You made a good suggestion. I never would have thought of that because I am so frustrated, I could die."

Miss Prova was the oldest resident on the block and had not been in good health. She had just gotten out of the hospital. No matter how she felt or how much time she had left, she loved her garden.

"I'm told that you are Miss Prova. I am just passing through. But I do have time to help you, if you share some ice water with me."

Miss Prova always had a jar of ice-cold lemonade when she worked in the garden.

"Well, it is not water, it is lemonade, and, yes, you can have some whether you help or keep moving on." She poured him a glass and gave him some of her famous teacakes.

The stranger and Miss Prova pulled out all the damaged zinnias and chrysanthemums and their roots. Together, they removed plants from the good beds and planted them on the north side. There were so many plants in the good beds that once they were finished, it did not appear that they had removed any from the good beds. The north side had become as full of plants as the good beds.

Miss Prova was a good Baptist and heavily involved in her church. She talked about her blessings and hummed hymns as they worked.

Something told her to put her glasses on. Now she could see the stranger.

She thought *why his hands were not as dirty as mine. Why did his shirt still have a fresh starched look? His bare feet were clean too.*

"But you've been walking in the dirt, just like me", she blurted out. "Who are you, mister?" The stranger did not answer. "If you won't answer, let me pay you for your time and you will have to leave."

"Miss Prova, thank you for the lemonade and the teacakes. That is payment enough from someone who loves the Lord as much as you do. You bring new beauty to God's flowers. You give them life. You have been worried about your health. Let me tell you that if you keep making beautiful flowers, you will live longer than all the adults on this block."

The stranger picked up a couple of teacakes and walked to the front of the house and out of sight. Miss Prova started after him. She wanted to pay him for his work. Her arthritis slowed her down. When she got to the front yard, the stranger was not in sight, but she did see George, Joe, and Moses in the front of their houses. They seemed to be looking for something. *But it could not be the stranger,* she thought.

After one week, the gardens around her house appeared as though there was never any damage from the flood and the contaminated canal. *They have never been this beautiful,* she thought. Moreover, so did the neighbors, as they could not stop complimenting Miss Prova on her garden. She could never tell her husband, Walter, that a white man had helped her. He would not understand. However, Walter believed the story she did tell, and she even testified to it in church.

Miss Prova often told a story that God saw how frustrated she was that her life's work was damaged and there was not much she could do to save it. Therefore, God sent her a guardian angel to watch over her and get her through transplanting the good plants. In addition, in the process, she gained new life for herself.

The Procession

On the Sunday following the appearance of the stranger, the Martins walked out of the house around 9:30 a.m., as usual. It happened to be a nice, clean, airy day, and the Gulf had not raised her dress yet. To the astonishment of the Martins most of the neighbors on the block were leaving their homes and walking to church. On a typical Sunday morning, only a few of the families in the 1100 block could be seen leaving the house and walking to church. Some went to the Catholic church, and others went to the Baptist church. If they started walking by 9:30 a.m., they would be on time for the ten a.m. service. Usually, it was the Beards, the Martins, Joyce, Mrs. Zeno, the Whites, and the Millers.

As they entered the oyster shell street, they could all see a procession of neighbors from the 900 to 1100 block converging southward to 9th Street, which led them to the church of their choice. They could also see neighbors from the 700 to 800 block converging northward to 9th Street. Everyone was dressed in their Sunday-go-to-meetings.

The scene reminded everyone of the May Procession by members of Sacred Heart Catholic Church each year. On the first Sunday in May, the Women's Auxiliary would dress in their white dresses, the Knights of Saint Peter Clavier in their dark suits, other ladies and young women in their latest Easter dresses, and most of the children in their white suits and dresses, which they wore for their First Communion earlier that day at Mass. They assembled at church and would parade up Washington Street to 7th Street, go west to Herget Street, turn eastward on 9th Street to Grannis Avenue and onto Gulfway Drive, turn south on Kansas Street to 10th Street, and then head back to the church at 10th and Washington. They would sing hymns honoring Mary, the Mother of Jesus Christ.

However, these neighbors were not sharing their experiences with one another. Everyone who might have been touched by the stranger that week on Welford Street was on their way to a church to praise God. *What was the reason all those families decided to go to church that Sunday?* After all, it was August; not Easter, not Christmas, not the first Sunday in May. Most of them knew the real reasons why they decided to go to church on this particular Sunday. The following Sunday did not have as many families walking to church. Years later, the stories would funnel through the neighborhood gossip channels and often cause a conversation to end for fear of revealing something that could classify them as applicants for the Rusk, Texas, crazy house.

Early Days

There were days in the thirties, forties, and fifties when the black kettles were steaming in most of the back-yards on Welford Street. In the thirties and forties, before soap was in the markets and made affordable, the residents on Welford made their own lye soap. They would render the fat from hogs, cattle, or sheep. Most of the fat could be obtained from the meat markets at no charge.

Neighborhood kids would go from yard to yard, watching and learning. On this day, Ms. Julia at 1146 was making soap. First, she would make the lye by leaching water through wood ashes. She packed ashes into a barrel with a hole in the bottom. Then she poured water on top, and it slowly trickled through the ashes. The lye dripping out at the bottom was a reddish brown-colored liquid, which can burn skin like acid. Lye was strong enough for making soap when a fresh egg would float in it. Then they would take scraps of fat trimmed off the meat during butchering. Fat was placed in a pot with a small amount of water and heated for several hours. She stirred the fat constantly to keep it from burning. It slowly melted down to a liquid form, and bits of meat and other impurities sunk to the bottom. When the fat was completely liquid, she set the pot aside to cool. As it cooled, the purified fat formed a solid layer on top with a layer of water and impurities at the bottom. She used hog fat or, as it is called, lard. Rendered fat and lye were boiled together in a pot to make soap. Salt was often added to separate excess lye and harden the soap. She poured the finished soap into a wooden box lined with damp cloth to cool and harden. Lye soap had to cure for several months before it could be used or it was too strong. The neighborhood women had to make soap on a monthly basis. The children would help the women and always seemed to get the word out that a kettle fire had started.

With all the children in the neighborhood and the daily dirty overalls from the men who worked at the refineries, the women would have to wash clothing six days a week. They could always be seen talking to each other from yard to yard as they hung or took down the daily wash.

In the forties, most backyards had a wash table, which had a manual clothes ringer attached. Wash tubs were positioned next to each other. One was used for scrubbing clothes on a washboard. A second, and sometimes third, tub was used for rinsing. One of these tubs had bluing in the rinse water.

Coincidentally, those tubs were also used to bathe children before there were bathtubs in the houses.

Women washing and hanging clothes in the backyard would have their Welford Street conversations across unfenced backyards. Every yard had clotheslines made with wooden or welded iron pipes connected by wire lines. Wooden clothespins held the clothing.

One day Ida Martin complained that her husband worked the graveyard shift and did not let her cook during the day.

"He keeps kicking me out of the kitchen," she told Julia and Joyce.

"I don't know what to do," Ida added.

"Send him to my house. I'll trade Emile," said Miss Julia, laughingly.

In the late forties, they were able to afford an electric washer that had a ringer attached to it. Many built a combination storage shed and wash house at the rear of the property. It was also in the late forties that Ida Martin asked her son Richard to go out back and ring out the clothes. Ida was sewing a dress in the living room when she thought she heard a voice saying, "See to your child". Then she heard Richard's screams come from the shed. She ran through the yard and found that he had his hand caught in the ringer and the rollers were turning. He had stuck his hand into the ringer through a window. His little body was hanging in mid-air, his tiptoes barely touching the ground. The ringer was holding his weight and grinding into his right hand. She lifted his body and tried to pull the hand free, but Richard only screamed louder. While holding him in one arm, she popped the release bar and his hand came free. The hand was bleeding and the brown skin had been rubbed off, revealing white flesh. Ida wrapped his hand with a towel from the rinse tub and consoled him.

Soon he was quiet. The sight of her little boy hanging out of the wash-shed window, as he appeared to be sucked in by the ringer-washer, was still on her mind.

She managed to get a ride from Elnora Beard to Doctor Gibson's office. In those days, Doc Gibson could not give appointments. The demand for medical attention was so great that it was on a first-come, first-served basis. You did not move to the front of the list unless you were bleeding or you had a broken bone protruding. Richard's hand had stopped bleeding but was severely raw. The office was steamy, crowded, and standing room only extended to the outside. It was a four-hour wait until Doc Gibson attended to Richard. There was no way he could have been seen earlier. Doc Gibson had to deliver a baby while they waited. Thousands of babies were born in that office, including Richard.

Mrs. Beard had waited with them and drove them home. Richard was her favorite child on the block and the godson of her sister, Elzina Wagner, who lived at 1038. Blackie, as she was called, was a light brown-skinned beauty and the most meticulously dressed woman in the neighborhood. Her husband, Dewey, worked at the Gulf. Elnora wanted to see where it happened. Ida took her and Richard to the shed. Blood signs were still on the ringer. The site caused Richard to tremble and run into the house. Ida and Elnora cleaned up everything. They moved the washer so that the ringer did not extend out of the window. Now no one would be reaching in through the window to the ringer, especially if it was turning the wrong way toward the washer and not outwards toward the rinse tub. Most of the sheds disappeared, as cars were affordable and garages needed to be built in the early fifties.

Every May, the Zenos, Martins, and Prevosts would order two or three dozen baby chicks through mail order. The *Spiegel* catalog was a big deal in those days. Women would look through the catalog at beautiful dresses and order patterns and sew their own dresses, which looked like those in *Spiegel*. Children would look at the toys and dream of ordering one day. Men would look at the tools, guns, and pretty models, dream, and then order baby chicks. The chicks would arrive in C.O.D. crates. They would raise them in pens, which were covered with chicken wire from top to bottom. This prevented them from flying away. They would allow some hens to hatch eggs, and those would grow to become fryers for the freezer.

Most kitchens had a stained floor or rotten wood area underneath the icebox because it was difficult to remember to empty the water tray. The tray would fill and flow onto the floor from the melting ice. Usually, when you stepped into water, you would empty the tray. In those days, they lived as Europeans by shopping daily and cooking it before it spoiled. Sometimes there would be a big cooking day and meat dishes prepared and stored in the icebox until they would be reheated and served. There was a fan in the icebox, which blew onto the block of ice and circulated cold air. The day before the iceman cometh was a day to shop at Plettman's Market downtown or Webb Grocery on Tenth Street near Welford. There were several of these two-room stores or corner markets throughout the west side. There were even houses where the homeowner turned the front room into a store replete with snacks, sodas, canned goods, and day-old bread. Many of these small stores were owned by Italians, Jews, and Cajuns. Most of the owners lived in a house attached or to the rear of the store. They associated with the Negroes on the west side, and some even attended the Sacred Heart Catholic Church.

Before they had freezers, they would hold the head in one hand and spin the chicken round and round until the neck snapped. Then they would drop the chickens and watch them flop on the ground. They would clean, cook, and eat the chicken on the same day. Once the Rich Plan freezers came to the neighborhood, they would kill all the fryer-sized chickens and freeze them. Each May, they would get more mail-order chicks regardless of how many laying hens they had. Eggs would be used for cooking.

Moses Martin made a mistake one year and was shipped two dozen turkey chicks. He had to build a separate coop for the turkeys. Eventually, he had to make a larger pen, so he slaughtered most of the chickens. He kept four laying hens and a rooster in a smaller area. The turkeys grew to enormous sizes. The largest gobbler weighed forty-four pounds cleaned. Moses had to saw it in half. It would not fit in the oven, in addition to being too much meat for his family on one holiday. That year, he served half on Thanksgiving and the other half on Christmas. Often, he gave many of the turkeys to family and needy families on Welford Street and the west side. The hens were hatching eggs, and the turkey crop never stopped. Some of the neighbors would buy feed from the Western Auto store and bring it to Moses. That guaranteed a turkey for their freezer. It seemed like there was an endless supply of turkey. Ida

knew numerous ways to prepare the meat. Turkey sand-
wiches every day in the kids' lunch boxes. Turkey and
gravy over rice, turkey soup, turkey dumplings, turkey
potpie, turkey fricassee, and turkey in eggplant dressing were a few of the menus for dinner in the Martin
household. Moses was the best cook in the household.
There was no doubt about it. He could fry fish, chicken,
and shrimp that restaurants could not match. He made
a special eggplant dressing that family members would
attempt to duplicate for decades, but none was exactly
as he made it taste. He made a banana nut cake that
family members would write and ask him to ship fro-
zen to them. Every Saturday, just like his mother, he
baked cakes. Eventually, this diet would lead to most
of the Martin family and other uncles, aunts, and cousins becoming diabetics. While the family members had
to start Insulin injections, the habit of eating delicious
food never stopped.

Martin Clan

Even though they were raised together, the Martin children chose very different routes in their development. Working at one of the refineries was not in the cards for them. They refused to follow in the footsteps of their parents, as would a majority of children on the west side.

Vincent, the oldest, who had been born with his left hand deformed, was always shy and quiet. He would endure teasing from the kids in the neighborhood and at Lincoln School. He could never play sports. He hardly ever was encouraged to believe that he was a normal kid. He would even be ridiculed by his own siblings. In his teenage years, Vincent spent a lot of time in Sabine Pass, Texas, with his aunt Ernestine Williams, his mother's oldest sister, and her husband, the gravedigger, Uncle Merrill. Vincent worked in Granger's Seafood Restaurant, the best in all of Texas, as a short-order cook during the summers. He was not teased or ridiculed in Sabine. He did not miss being on Welford Street.

The Martins would visit often, especially when Uncle Merrill would slaughter a hog. He raised a lot of eight hundred-plus-pound hogs. He would drive around to houses and food businesses and collect discarded food, or "slop", as it was called. He would add water and some grain to the mixture to feed the hogs. He had a large wood-burning stove and oven on his back porch. The smell of the sweet wood smoke had permeated the wooden walls on his porch. He would cook the pork in and on that stove and make some of the most delicious pork around town. The Williams family shared the meat with family and friends.

The Martins would always return to Port Arthur with meat from Uncle Merrill and seafood from Aunt Ernestine. Many of their neighbors worked in the fishing industry and would trade seafood for pork.

Since Sabine Pass was a seaport town, Vincent would make the right connections during his summer jobs, which led to him becoming a merchant seaman and galley chef. His life was spent on the oceans, where he gained respect from his siblings and overcame the embarrassment he had about his hand while growing up. He married Ella and had two sons: Vincent, Jr. and Bryant. He bought a home and lived a good life until he developed lung cancer from years of heavy smoking and died in 1998.

Rosita, or Rody, as she was nicknamed, was a popular young girl. She had taken piano lessons from Mrs. Mitchell on 8th and Herget Street. For all that she was able to get her parents to do for her; one would have thought she was an only child. She would fill the house with beautiful sounds whenever she played. This was encouraging to the Martin children, who learned that they could accomplish most anything. Watching Rody learn the piano and move on to playing classics gave them inspiration.

Rody was also a starter on the Lincoln High School basketball team. That was when girls played with six players. Three girls were on each side of the half-court line, three girls were on defense, and three girls were on offense. They could not cross the half-court line.

In her Jr. Year, she was featured in a parade with a box over her head to her waist, which was decorated like a bumblebee, the school mascot, and showed off her legs. She had the best pair of legs at the school as voted by the student body. She was so popular that she was chosen as Miss Lincoln and the homecoming queen her senior year.

Rody went off to Prairie View A&M College. In her second semester, she became pregnant. Moses and Ida were embarrassed, but after the baby girl, Margaret was born in November, they raised her and sent Rody back to complete college. She would not make that mistake again. She obtained her degree in teaching at Paul Quinn College in Waco and later got her master's at Wisconsin University.

She became a teacher, married a local man, and had two more children, Ida, named after her mother, and Byron. She would later divorce and move to Carson, California, to teach and marry a former classmate.

Growing up, Maurice was the bully in the family. He would rather pick a fight than play. He was feared, and kids did not pick on the other Martin children. Although, through the navy, he traveled to all continents in the world, he would settle in Port Arthur because every time he went home on leave, he felt the ties that bind.

He was the hunter. He loved to hunt and fish. Early on, he would build box traps to catch blackbirds in the backyard. He would tie a brick to a box and place a stick under one side to prop it up. He placed chicken feed under and around the box. He tied a line of twine to the stick and would camp out on the back porch near an open window. When there were four or more birds under the box, he would pull the string. He would run to the box, reach in, and break the necks of each bird. When he had done this enough to get about twenty birds or a mess of them, he would clean them, season them, and bake them. Later, after he had earned money as a paperboy, he bought a BB gun and abandoned trapping birds for shooting them.

He would help care for Mr. Walter Zeno's dogs and get to go on real rabbit hunts with real shotguns. Hunting kept him out of trouble for many years. He would use his father's .410-gauge shotgun. He would remember the day his father brought home an automatic .16-gauge Browning and handed him a payment book. Then he told him, "If you want to be a good hunter, you need a real gun. And you need to pay for it."

It would be a few hunts later that his father would allow him to use the new shotgun. He had to break it in first. On the other hand, as Maurice thought, he really wanted a good gun for himself but used Maurice to pay for it.

He did not like sports. He liked to go fishing and crabbing at the Pleasure Pier, which was an island just south of the Intra-coastal Canal. To get to the pier, one had to go through downtown and cross over the drawbridge. It was a good walk. He rode the bike that he used to deliver the *Port Arthur News*. There he was with his rod and reel, bait box, and a croaker sack with neck bones and string to use for crabbing. He was never alone. There were always other boys on their way to do the same. On a good day, he had to push the loaded bike all the way home.

He and his friends would even go exploring at Alligator Bend, which was only thirteen blocks from 1100 Welford. The bend was located behind Carver Elementary School. The city had built a new school out near the swampy area of the west side. Kids were pelted by mosquitoes on a daily basis. In addition, it was too close to the Gulf refinery and the railroad tracks, which served the grain docks, refineries, and ship offloading. There were real alligators in the bend. Maurice and his buddies used to go swimming there. Often, they would have to make a run for it. One of his friends drowned in the bend. For a long time after that, he stayed away from swimming there but not from exploring or running a hound dog to chase rabbits.

Kids in the neighborhood used to explore what was called the dump. A levy was built when the refineries dredged a canal, which soon became contaminated with oil residue. The dump ran parallel with Foley Street and would later be paved and then concreted and named MLK Drive.

Maurice graduated from Lincoln in 1959 and joined the navy. He would marry and have two children with Patricia from Norfolk, Virginia, where he was based. He traveled the world and even saw time in Vietnam. They supplied the Swift boats, which were in the news so much during the election of 2004. Moses would visit Maurice in Virginia, and they would go deer hunting. His guardian angel was looking after him on a hunting trip when he was shot by another hunter. They were using shotguns with slugs, or buckshot, in the shell casings. That was the law in that state: No rifles allowed. They also used dogs to round up and chase deer into clearings where hunters could get a good shot. The hunter who shot Maurice did not follow procedure and fired toward the woods rather than through the clearing. He missed the deer and hit Maurice. Three glancing buckshot and superficial wounds put him in the hospital. Maurice had never seen his father so upset; he had threatened to kill the hunter. Maurice had never heard him curse before, but the words that came out of his father's mouth that day would never be heard from him again until the day he died. He berated the hunter something fierce. Maurice got him to calm down so they could get to the car and drive to a hospital. Maurice always felt that he was blessed, because if the hunter had used a slug, and it had hit him anywhere in the center of his body and exploded, he could have died.

He retired from the navy after twenty years, divorced Patricia, went to college, and married Belinda. They had a son while living in Mississippi. He moved to Port Arthur, divorced Belinda, and years later married a high school sweetheart, Diane.

He settled down to merchant shipping, buying rental property, fishing, and hunting. He decided to finish college and taught school. That would last only until he got the urge again. His sea legs were always stronger than his land legs. He would go back to sea again and again.

He received an accommodation from the US government for participating in the delivery of military vehicles and equipment to the Iraq war zone. The Turkish government would not allow the ships to offload in their ports. The ships had to circumnavigate to Kuwait, where they delivered their cargo. He decided after that trip that, being over sixty, he was too old for that kind of work. He jumped ship, flew home from Amsterdam, and went back to hunting and fishing.

Growing up, Barbara, the fifth child, spent a lot of time with her Nan-Nan (godmother), who was a married daughter of the Prevost family at 1146. She began kindergarten at four years of age. The Sacred Heart School principal said that she knew enough to start going to school. She went on to make her First Communion and Confirmation, as did all the other Martin children. She would remember her daddy fixing lunches for all of his children except on Fridays, because lunch at school was tuna on a bun with potato chips. That was her favorite school lunch food. Recess was a highlight for everyone because they got to play basketball in the courtyard. Girls played on one half of the court and boys on the other. They never played games with the boys. The nuns saw to that. The only interaction at this Catholic school would be in plays and operettas.

In high school, the nuns would sponsor and chaperone square dance nights. They taught boys and girls how to square dance during the day. You could not pick your partner. The nuns did. You might wind up with the ugliest boy or the dumbest boy. However, it all worked out evenly, as you would get to partner with every boy. Square dances were held on Saturday nights, and there was a strict dress code. Girls had to wear below-knee wide skirts and white blouses, and boys could wear khaki pants or blue jeans with a white shirt. If they broke a sweat, they knew they were having fun. She had great respect for the nuns and priest that were over them. They really made her believe that they were the next step to God's heavenly place. Each school day would begin with prayer. One of the prayers was to guardian angels. It was also taught at home by her mother. Barbara prayed it aloud, saying, "Angel of God, My Guardian Dear, to whom God's love commits me here. Ever this day be at my side, to light and guard and rule and guide. Amen."

She graduated in 1962 and enrolled at Prairie View College. She majored in nursing. She completed one semester. There must have been something about young girls in their first year at this college. She did not learn from her sister's mistakes at PV. She had to marry Robert James, a resident of Port Arthur, who had served three years in the military. They would have four children: Mavis, Rodrick, Angela, and Rhonda. This union was subjected to divorce seven and a half years later. She went on to raise the children alone. Years later, she would forgive Robert and encourage her daughters to allow him into their lives. She was able to get a job at St. Mary's Hospital in data processing after attending a business school in Beaumont. She was not paid the best, but God and her guardian angel were with her. Her children went on to be survivors in this world. Her three daughters were military veterans. She always encouraged them to get all that she had missed out on. Eventually, it paid off for most of them. There were twenty-five years as a single mother. In a friendly relationship, she got pregnant and wanted the child. She gave birth to Raiford. She did not want to marry his father. Raiford was the baby of the family, and everyone agreed that he was a spoiled brat who was loved by everyone he met. Years later, Barbara would look back and be able to count twelve grandchildren and one great-grandchild. She met and married John Nico. She is still learning true values about life and making vows before God. She never forgot the guardian angel prayer. She would retire from St Mary's Hospital in 2003.

Anthony grew up in the shadow of his older brothers, especially Richard. He would be compared to "Mo", as Richard had been nicknamed during high school after his father, Moses. Giving someone a nickname formulated after their father's name or something inherent to their father was begun as a way of teasing each other. There were names like Fanwell, Duddy, Cut Toe, Energy, Norman, Vivian, P.W., many others, and, of course, Mo. Anthony played on the Sacred Heart basketball team. Still, there were the Mo standards to live up to. Anthony liked art. As a teenager, he sent away for one of the art kits that were advertised in comic books and *Look* magazines during that time. He would go on to graduate from Lamar University in Commercial Art. He taught school in Port Arthur for nearly two years. He tired of that, especially after a failed relationship with a young woman he had met while working as a teacher. He joined the Peace Corps and spent two years in Africa. He learned about the African cultures and was able to teach many children and adults how to paint and draw. During his stay, he completed hundreds of drawings and numerous paintings of Africans and the scenery. He would settle in Colorado Springs near Denver and later in Aurora. Anthony was forever attending college. He will not admit how many degrees he holds. Should he be called doctor? Does he have his doctorate? Only he knows. He remained distant from most of his siblings with the exception of Rody. He continued to stay in contact with her. Anthony never married. After all, the Martin children, except for Vincent and Althea, had married more than once. Everyone resolved that he was just a confirmed bachelor. There were never any girlfriends to talk about after the Peace Corp stint. Being alone in Africa and concentrating on his volunteer work and the solace he encountered while painting his art works formulated a desire to never marry. Whenever Moses and Ida or other family members would visit him, Anthony was the expert Colorado host and always showed family a good time on his tours.

Carl had to live up to the Mo legacy, also. In fact, he inherited the nickname. He grew up the sibling that was forever holding onto his mother's leg. She would have to drag him around the house as she did her cleaning and cooking. Picture a marsupial with a pouch; if Ida Martin would have had a pouch, then Carl would have been in it. He was the baby for nine years until the birth of Althea. Carl grew up without having the protection of older brothers to defend him, as Richard and

Anthony had, because the older boys were now out of the house, living their own lives. He had to fight on his own in the neighborhood. One day, three boys jumped Carl and started beating him with sticks and a two-by-four board, which had nails in it. Before Mrs. White at 1100 Welford could stop them, Carl had been hit in the head with the board and almost lost consciousness. Those boys took off running down Eleventh Street when Mrs. White lashed into their midst. She took care of Carl and brought him home. None of those thugs would have singly tried to mix it with Carl. It took three of them and sticks and boards.

That blunt trauma to his head would surface in the future when he would be operated on for a brain aneurysm. When Carl graduated from high school, he went to live with Richard in Dallas and attended Bishop College. When Richard moved to California, Carl stayed in Dallas, lived on campus, and later joined the coast guard. He would marry Joyce and have a son. After their divorce, he would meet Sylvia Martin (no relation) through a Baptist church. She had recently been widowed. She had a young daughter, Tonya. Carl and Sylvia had another girl and a boy, Tiffany and Courtney, and would adopt another boy, Justin, when their two were twelve and ten. Years later, they would adopt three more abandoned children they saw while watching a Tuesday's Child TV special. Carl worked in helicopter and Learjet plants for many years. He was forced into medical retirement at an early age after he hurt his back at work. He was real active in his church and later began a ministry in preaching. Carl had major operations on his spine and, years later, one for a brain aneurism. Both had miracle recoveries. In his medi-cal retirement, he would go on to become a patented inventor and then a talk show host on radio and Black cable TV. The title of his show was "The Many Faces of a Black Man."

When Ida Martin passed forty, she figured child-bearing was behind her. However, she became preg-nant in 1958. She wanted Althea because it would keep her young. She had just spent the year before raising Rody's daughter, Margaret, her first grandchild. Here she was at forty-one, believing she was going through early menopause. Truth is, she learned there would be another baby in the house. Most of the family did not believe she should be having a baby at her age. Her sis-ters attempted to talk her out of it. Some relatives and friends were embarrassed to be seen with her, includ-ing her own children. Richard did not mind taking her places because he got to drive. Her children soon learned from her that they should not be embarrassed by God's will. Richard became Althea's godfather. Althea grew up almost as an only child. All of her siblings had left home by the time she was ten years old. Moses and Ida allowed her to be spoiled. She was able to get all that she wanted within their means. She was the first daughter to take dance lessons. She would be involved in the band in high school after having taken music lessons. She went on to Lamar University for nearly four years.

Althea and her college friends liked to drink alcohol. Times had changed in Port Arthur, and the culture of the youth had come along with the times. When Moses decided to clamp down and she would not stop, he cut her money stream off. With thirty semester hours to graduate, she rebelled, quit college, and joined the army. She married a boyfriend who was into drugs. He traveled with her to Germany, and there they had two girls. Her husband was forever in trouble and jeopardized her career in the army. He was sent home. She had to raise the girls alone. They eventually divorced. In 1987, when Moses died, she came home from Germany. Barbara had moved into 1146 after the Prevosts had all passed away and their grandson rented the house. Most of the out-of-town siblings stayed with Barbara and Maurice.

Moses' death, in March of 1987, was sudden and unexpected. He had been working in his beloved garden in the backyard, tending to his okra and tomato plants, when he heard the telephone in the house ringing. He had been waiting for Ida to call to tell him that she was ready to be picked up from the hospital, where she had been for a week. Moses ran into the house and slipped on a throw rug, causing him to fall on his back and hit his head. Ida called Maurice and Vincent, who lived in Port Arthur during those years, to check on their father. They found Moses still on the kitchen floor. They got him up and sped to the same hospital where Ida was waiting. Moses died of a brain hemorrhage that night.

All the children came home for the funeral. Eleven Thirty-six had been remodeled and enlarged so Barbara could move in and share the home with Ida. When Althea got out of the army, she moved into 1136 with Barbara and Ida. Anthony had offered for her and her daughters to come to Colorado and live with him. Anthony felt that Althea would be able to get a good job and eventually move out on her own. After a visit,

Althea decided to move back into 1136. Friction in 1136 caused Barbara to move out. Family members believed that Ida Martin wanted to join Moses but did everything to better her failing health in order to provide housing and assistance for Althea and her daughters. Joy had graduated, and Cabrina was a senior in high school. It was not until May 2003 that Ida would give up on staying alive. She had been in a nursing home for the last twelve months and had begun to not recognize her family. She had stopped talking to family members. She would utter a few words to one special nurse's aide. Richard, Carl, Barbara, and some of their children went to visit Ida. The nurse rolled her to the front window so she could see outside. They all gathered around a large table. She would not speak nor hold eye contact with anyone. Then Richard took a hospital folder and wrote on it: *Who is that?* He put it in front of Ida and pointed to Barbara. She tried to mutter some words. Then he pointed to Carl. In addition, she muttered, "Carl". She smiled. Then Richard pointed to Catherine, his wife, and Ida shouted, "Cathy". Soon she named everyone he pointed to. Then Richard wrote *would you like to go visit 1136?*

Ida read it out loud. "Would you like to go visit 1136?" And she added, "*Right now!*"

"Well, I'll be John Brown", Carl said.

"No, you are not. You are Carl," Ida said in a raised voice.

Everyone cheered this change and hugged her. She smiled, laughed, and kept saying "right now".

Barbara arranged for the nurse to clean her up and dress her for the visit. Ida could not stop telling everyone she saw on the way to her room that she was going to 1136. No one knows whether she talked to the angel that day, but a week after returning to the nursing home, she stopped talking again. Her skin cleared, she had a youthful look to her face, and then she rested.

Richard's Journey

I was the fourth child and the brother that Maurice picked on until I outgrew him. It seemed like it happened one summer after I spent three months on my uncle Alfonse's farm. His wife, Aunt Alice, ran the farmhouse, and he ran the ranch for the Dishmans. The Dishmans were a family who had free slaves to whom they sold parcels of land and were obligated to work for hire on his ranch and in his rice paddies. I was fourteen years old when I arrived home and had grown three inches. I was six feet three inches and towered over everyone in the Martin family. The next year, I grew to six feet five inches. My family chided me that the only reason I grew so tall because I walked barefoot in cow manure. Well, that is not exactly what they said.

In actuality, I think it was because my mother's Mitchell genes kicked in, doing the hard farmwork, drinking fresh milk, and eating fresh food that my aunt Alice cooked every meal. Now, since I was a lot taller, I was Maurice's pal. No more spats between us. There

was no more arguing about wearing clothes. Maurice's
pants did not fit me anymore. We even went on hunting trips together with our dad and Mr. Zeno. We went
fishing and crabbing a lot at the pier. There was also
some night fishing for garfish at the pier. We would
use a frog gig (an open clamp that locked onto the
subject) mounted on a broomstick, which was tied to a
rope. When the tide rolled out at night, the garfish (it
really does taste like chicken) would get caught in the
shallows, and Maurice and I would gig them and pull
them onto the bank by the rope. Then it would take a
big blow to its head to kill it. Getting a thirty or forty
pounder home was a chore. Some were as big as one
hundred pounds.

I was considered the lucky Martin. I had the best
godmother, and other neighbors always gave me things.
They also taught me to drive, and I would drive them
around town on their errands or doctor visits. At age
four, I won a big drawing at the Hollywood theater
where we would go to watch a movie every Saturday
for ten cents. We grew up on newsreel reports of the
war, Lash La Rue, Tom Mix, Roy Rogers, Cisco Kid
(and Pancho), "The Little Rascals," and cartoons. All
the kids on the west side were at the theater that day.
I had the winning ticket for a tricycle. Everyone in the
neighborhood was jealous. Another older kid named
Blondie won the grand prize of a live Shetland pony.

Having grown so tall, I would become a basketball
star at Sacred Heart High. In fact, our Sacred Heart
team won the Texas Catholic Interscholastic State
Championship in 1959, 1960, and 1961. The team was
so good that Black college freshmen teams put us on

their schedule. There were late-night visits to scrimmage in uniform against Texas Southern University and Prairie View A&M College. Both games had official timekeepers and referees but only a few fans in the stands. Only the lights over the court were on. The exterior building lights did not announce that something was going on in the gym. There was a good reason. There would be no publicity telling the whipping we put on those freshmen teams. The top public high school teams in Houston took note after Sacred Heart played perennial state finalists Wheatley, Jack Yates, and Kashmere from Houston, Texas.

Our team should have been rated in the top five in the USA. High school teams were not rated, as they would be in the future. Games were four eight-minute quarters, and it was rare that the Sacred Heart Red Raiders did not score over one hundred points in a game. I was there for the first two state championship years and graduated in 1960.

High school course study came easy to me. I took notes in class, which made it easy for me to pass all the weekly exams. I overheard two nuns talking in the library one day about the methods that college students used in class. I tried it, and it worked for me. I would later wish that I had studied much harder. Our principal was a nun whose brother was a dean at Notre Dame University. She counseled me in my senior year and told me how I should apply myself, and if she saw those recommended changes, she would help me get a scholastic scholarship to Notre Dame.

I tried to change, but basketball and girls were taking more of my time. After all, I had learned how to get

A's and not have to study much. The principal called me to her office and told me that she would have to talk to my parents in order to get me to follow her study recommendations. I was unnerved and told her to keep her scholarship. I would have other offers and did not need her help. Years later, I would try to kick my own rear for having made the wrong decisions. I could have attended Notre Dame. However, after high school, I enrolled at Lamar Tech in Beaumont and majored in chemical engineering. My sister Barbara, Anthony, and I would be the only Martins to graduate from the Catholic school.

I was dating my high school sweetheart, Helen, who had gone to live in Houston while attending a business school. Helen had to have an operation and came home in May of 1961.

I learned that I had not been prepared in high school for chemical engineering. My grades were not A's and B's in my second semester, so I decided to join the army in May. Training was easy for me following a first-place finish in the Fort Hood Steeplechase. I had not planned on running, but I was told to enter by my training sergeant. I found myself coming from the back of the pack, up and down the hilly course, through the woods, over fences, over streams, until I had the leaders in sight. I saw a fence, and on the other side was a small stream. Having long jumped in track, I leaped over the fence and landed on the far edge of the stream, passing the leaders. There was one officer who, as I learned later, ran long distance in college, was sprinting to the finish line. I made a dramatic sprint to pass him and win the steeplechase. That accomplishment would help me get into army sports during my term of service. After boot camp, I came home for a two-week leave and fell right into a planned wedding. I married Helen. We had talked about marriage on the telephone and in letters. I never formally proposed to her. However, when I arrived in Port Arthur, all I had to do was get a tuxedo and ask six friends to get a tux and join me in the wedding. Helen, her family, and my parents had done all the arranging. Even our honeymoon had no frills. It was a trip in the Martin family station wagon to Lafayette, Louisiana, where my aunt Alma and Uncle Oris welcomed us. Aunt Alma had her house full of neighbors and relatives who all expected to see us in white gown and tuxedo. We were not hungry but had to eat because there was enough to feed my army platoon.

I went back to Fort Hood after those two weeks and lived in the barracks until I could find a place for Helen and me to live. Six months later, we shared a two-bedroom house with a couple from Kansas City, Kansas.

My work life in the army brought me skills in personnel and office administration. I was in charge of commissioned officer efficiency reporting. I had a top-secret clearance because of the personal information I was exposed to on all of the 2d Armored Division officers. Each officer coming in or transferring out had to visit with me as I processed all of their transfers, promotions, and musters. I was part of Operation Big Lift in 1963. President Kennedy wanted to show the world that a military division could be moved from the USA to Europe in record time. In a time span of sixty-four hours from the first C-135 propeller airplane that left Kelly Air Base in Texas to the last plane arriving in Germany established the record. I spent twenty-one days in France and Germany before flying back in a jetliner, which took eight hours. President Kennedy was scheduled to attend a parade and pass in review by the Big Lift Division at Fort Hood. We had practiced and on November 22nd, 1963, went to work in our dress uniforms, only to be told that the parade was cancelled. The president would not be coming to Fort Hood. A decision was made to give us the day off, since we were not dressed in fatigues. I went home, undressed, and was sitting in front of the TV when the news alerts started about President Kennedy being shot in Dallas. I often wondered who the person was who decided to cancel the president's trip to Fort Hood. If the Warren Commission could have found out who made that decision, that is who was responsible for his assassination.

After my honorable discharge from military service, I moved back home to 1136 Welford. Mother invited me to stay because Helen was expecting with our second child. There was one room where the three of us could sleep.

There was always something good about going home and living on that block. I registered with employment agencies and completed government applications the same week I arrived home. I took the post office examination and aced it. Normally, there would be months to wait before the post office would call you for part-time work. However, within ten days after the exam, I got the call. I worked at the post office in Port Arthur as a distribution clerk and volunteered for overtime to deliver mail and sometimes work as a cashier at the branch office in midtown. After three months, I bought our first house and moved out of 1136. Our second son had been born a month earlier. I could not understand all the good fortune that was coming to me and my family. Later in life, it would all be explained and exposed. I used the skills from the military to become an assistant to the postmaster. He had very little office management experience and depended on me to process all of the administrative functions. This exposure would be the basis for the Dallas, Texas, postal region manager to invite me to transfer to the region office for the USPO in Dallas. I would work on land leases and building leases for all postal facilities in Texas and Oklahoma. Then I became the first Black new-car salesperson in the city of Dallas. That would bring me some noto-riety in the Black community. I became well known in the city of Dallas, not just in the Black community, but through a Black professional organization named National Association of Market Developers (NAMD), I met and became friends with all of the key Black sales representatives for major corporations.

My younger brother, Carl, would come to live with me and attend Bishop College. I was active in Saint Joseph Catholic Church. So much so, that I was appointed the church's Apostle of Good Will represen-tative to the Diocese. Our NAMD chapter attended the funeral of Martin Luther King and later visited the memorial while our national convention was being held in Atlanta.

One Sunday in October of 1968, I was seated at my desk in the classroom of the Confraternity of Christian Doctrine School of Holy Cross Catholic Church in Dallas, Texas. I reflected on my physician's examination of two days before. I had been told that I had from one to two years to live. I had contracted a terminal form of bladder cancer. I could not afford to get a second opinion, although I wanted to, because I really felt healthy. I recalled the feeling that came over me when my doctor and friend advised that my life would be close to normal most of the time and that medication would only prolong the inevitable.

I did not want Helen to know about my condition. I was assured by my friend, Dr. Prince, that he would leave that task up to me. He advised me that the sooner I would consult her, the easier Helen would take the shock. At this point, I was in the deepest of thought, embracing the notion that I should consult the Almighty first as I began to pray to God for guidance and a guardian angel to assist in my plight to prepare for my family's security after I was gone. I would daily ask God to extend my order that I could provide a financial and spiritual legacy for my children. I would ask Him to help me accomplish now what I had been putting off until then—*then* being a time in the future, because I believed that I would live for a long time.

My Confraternity of Christian Doctrine (CCD) class started walking in for their religious instructions. I did not answer their greetings, and the students felt dejected and wondered to themselves if they had done something wrong to their favorite CCD teacher on the last Sunday. There had been an examination, and today they were to learn of their results. I kept my head bowed until one of the students touched me on the shoulder and asked, "Mr. Martin, you haven't answered. Did we lose out last week? Did we all fail the test?"

I came to myself and realized that my entire class had seated themselves. They were ready to begin class studies. A tear ran down my cheek as I raised my head, and a little Hispanic girl pulled a tissue out of the box on my desk, and caused me to simultaneously place my hand on her shoulder, saying, "God is here, and he has helped all of you pass the test."

She dried my tear.

"And that is what I am so happy about. I realize that He has blessed me and enabled me to bring His Word to you and all of you can use it in your everyday lives."

I asked her to be seated and then began to speak from my heart on a prepared text from the lesson plan. I told the class I had one desire, which was for all of the church's children, especially this class, to be saturated with the Word of God, and they would gain an all-surpassing knowledge of Jesus Christ.

"It can hardly be necessary for me to remind you that the most valued treasure of every family library and the most frequently and lovingly made use of book should be the Holy Bible."

Surprisingly, I began to recite from a Bible verse I had read the night before.

Show me, O Lord, my life's end and the number of my days; let me know how fleeting is my life. You have made my days a mere handbreadth; the span of my years is as nothing before you. Each man's life is but a breath. Man is mere phantom as he goes to and fro: He bustles about, but only in vain; he heaps up wealth, not knowing who will get it. But now, Lord, what do I look for? My hope is in you.

Psalms 39:4 -7, NIV

As I continued the lesson, the students appeared more moved than ever before as I prepared to dismiss them. They had often reported to the parish priest of the teacher's love they possessed for Mr. Martin. I had wanted to talk about death, preparation, and the importance of being faithful to God because you never know when your time will come, but these were young children, and that was the wrong message for them. Yet I felt that I had been given the opportunity to fully prepare for my soul and to make reparations and give penance for my past. However, I realized that every man is conscious of death and has a chance to prepare himself, though the time may be longer.

I asked my students to sit in the front pews and sing out during the Mass and to say their prayers loudly to encourage the entire congregation to join in their examples.

Walking down the hallway toward the vestibule of the church with the girls and boys, I greeted parents of the students who had often waited to accompany their children to Mass. I could sense the feeling the parents had for me because I had made their plight easier by teaching catechism to their children.

One of the parents, Brad Morgan, was a friend. Brad was employed by Humble Oil Company. Standard Oil of New Jersey, the richest corporation in the world, was its parent company. It was the biggest and most respected in Texas. The company hired the best personnel in its operations. David Hunt, another Humble Oil friend of mine, had influenced the hiring of Brad away from Hamm's Brewery, where Brad had been a sales representative. They were in the marketing department.

They were both members in the local chapter of the NAMD, of which I had been elected as treasurer. Brad told me that he wanted to talk to me after the Mass.

I was also a Mass lector and had to prepare myself for the readings and literature before the Mass began. I honestly felt that my students, who sang as though they were angels, were there to comfort me. During the Mass, I prayed for assistance and guidance in finding the vehicle by which I could prepare for my family after I was gone.

Usually I would receive congratulations from the parishioners for my performance as lector after the Mass ended, and this day was not different. I always added emphasis to the often-drab words in the Catholic missal readings. I stopped on my way to meet Brad and made a visit to Father Joe Weinsaphl to receive a blessing. I told the priest that something tragic had happened and that I would need counseling. While Father Joe encouraged me to tell him what had happened, I was not ready to talk about it, and I told him that I would see him next Saturday afternoon.

Brad Morgan was talking to one of the parishioners, Mrs. Davis, and she was talking as I walked up to them.

"I saw a commander's application come through the office on you, so you are going to work for my company?"

"I didn't know you worked there, Mrs. Davis," Brad responded.

Overhearing the conversation, I broke in and spoke to Brad.

"Are you leaving Humble Oil, Brad?"

"I may leave them, Richard, and that's what I wanted

to talk to you about. You see, David asked me to have you come to his house after Mass."

"You are not trying to get Mr. Martin to go to work there too, are you?" Mrs. Davis asked.

"He might get me to go to work if it is a better company than Humble Oil. What kind of company is it, Brad?"

Mrs. Davis spoke up before Brad had a chance.

"Insurance," she emphatically said.

I spoke up with a sort of defiance.

"Man, no. I'll never go to work for an insurance company."

"Let me give both of you some advice," Mrs. Davis warned. "I work for this company because I have to and because I've been there for seven years and during which time I've seen a many good men come and go. Now, if you decide to go with them, I wish you the best of luck," she said as she walked away.

"What is this all about, Brad?" I asked.

Brad responded. "Do you want to make more money than you ever expected to make? No, don't answer that yet. I want you to talk to David so he can tell you more about it."

"I don't see that we have anything to talk about, Brad. I'm not interested in calling on people in their homes. I like selling, but I prefer direct selling to businesses or to entrepreneurs."

"This is not really selling, Richard, and it is not really insurance, but just meet me over at David's for a few minutes and you'll see why I made $250 yesterday and really didn't work for it."

"Two hundred and fifty dollars!" I exclaimed.

"Yes, that's right. How much have you earned in one day?"

"About $135 when I sold three cars in a day," I explained.

"Okay, then I'll meet you at David's in thirty minutes and he can explain how it works."

When I was behind the wheel of my car on the way home, I envisioned this being the opportunity I needed to secure my family's future and that maybe God had answered my requests.

I really wanted to know more about David leaving Humble Oil to go to an insurance company because, as I recalled, David had worked for an insurance company and had failed. I remembered him saying that he would never go to work for an insurance company. This is why I wanted to talk to him; because I knew David had done a great job for the oil company and was about ready for a promotion. I also knew David was a smart man and that this new business opportunity had to be something good to lure him away from Humble Oil Company, which he often demonstrated he would fight a man in defense of it if he uttered false words against Humble.

He was a boastful sort of fellow, and I thought back to the time when there was a rumor going around Dallas that the *In Sepia* newspaper publisher, Tony Davis, was going to call a boycott in the Black areas against Humble Oil service stations. David did not sleep for nights until he gained nerve enough to confront Tony, only to learn it was just a rumor.

Boy, was he relieved, I remembered.

I arrived home, and my two oldest sons met me in the driveway. I explained to Helen that David had asked me to come over for a few minutes, and I was going to take the family for a ride after lunch.

"What does he want that can't wait until after lunch?" Helen asked.

"He wants to talk about some insurance company he is working for about a job or something."

"Now, Richard, do you remember I told you I would leave you if you left the job you have now," she said, seemingly kidding.

I assured her that I was not leaving my job and talk was all that would transpire.

"I'll be back within the hour."

I loved my wife and family and knew how waiting to tell them about my condition was not fair. I prayed as I traveled to David's and asked if David's wanting to talk to me was the answer to my needs. As I approached his house, I noticed David and Brad standing in the driveway.

"Hold it, Richard. Let us in. We want you to drive us someplace while we talk!" shouted David with his deep, commanding voice.

They got into my Ford XL convertible and, as I was driving, they fed me directions, not telling me where we were going. I stopped on the Loop 12 roadside and let the top down on the car.

David leaned over the console from the backseat and stated, "Richard, I asked you to come by because I am making money, lots of money, and I want you to have the same opportunity. Now don't say a word until I'm through, okay? Head on Loop 12, then north on the Central Expressway. Richard, you know John Hooper, my supervisor with Humble, and you know me. John has given me the same chance I am going to give you, a chance to make a thousand dollars a week. I made one thousand dollars last week in bonuses alone. I won a $1500 tie tack, a $350 Rolex watch, and this is it here. I have got one hundred-dollar bills in my pocket, which I have never had before. Edith, my wife, won a $1200 diamond watch and a two hundred-dollar broach, and I was given a fifty-dollar Countess Mara necktie. Now show him the money you won, Brad, and here is mine."

They began to flash hundred-dollar bills, fifties, and twenties. One twenty-dollar bill got caught in a wind gust because the top was down and flew onto the expressway.

"Whoa, how much was that?" shouted Brad.

"I think it was a twenty. Could have been a hundred, but don't worry. I hope someone who really needs it will find it. There is more to be made from where that came from," replied David with his usual boastful laugh.

I was impressed to say the least, in addition to being overwhelmed by this display of soundness and confidence in both of them, and my first reply was, "This racket you say you're in, is it honest?" "I am in public relations with Great National Life Insurance Company and we place, not sell, institutional contracts, and that's what we make money on."

"Institutional?" I queried.

"Yes, what we're doing is giving mainly professional people an opportunity to invest with protection for their money, coverage on their life for the benefit of their families, and 30 percent returns on their investment, which grows with interest and dividends each and every year. And furthermore, you missed your turn.

Get off at the next exit. We've got some Humble Oil season tickets to the Cowboys football game."

My first thought was back to Helen's lunch. It should be ready. I did not tell them about my promise to be right back.

David went on to explain how he had heard about this company from John Hooper, who encouraged him to leave the oil company, and how Brad won his money as a commander with the company. They explained that a commander was a center of influence that led an associate like David to the right people. It sounded too good to be true, and I told them I would need to know more. That was when Brad stated he was going to join the company as an associate.

David continued and told me that the company asks three things of an associate: to work hard, follow instructions given, and the third, which really caught my attention and my heart, was to tithe to the church of his choice.

He stated that the company was headed by a Christian-oriented president who wanted to do something for all people. David also felt that under Steed's direction, the company had become Christian oriented.

The president, Mr. Ronald Steed, was handicapped as a child and could not speak or hear until he was nine. The Methodist church in East Texas had sent him to a hospital and he was cured, although he still had a slight speech impediment. Steed then went through life doing good for people and built this insurance company to help share the profits of a company in the most lucrative business in the world. David also stated that he had met personally with Mr. Steed, who said that all of the men he brought to the company would be managers soon and would make more money than they ever believed possible.

About this time, we had arrived at the Cotton Bowl stadium. I had almost made up my mind to join too. I remembered one other thing, which David said, that I could not get off my mind. That was Steed's instructions for each associate to tithe from his earnings. At this point, I did not know who the Cowboys were playing or who won the game.

I was really thinking about all of the things my friend had said. I trusted Brad's opinion, and I decided to learn in order to ascertain this to be the answer I was in search of to leave a financial legacy for my family.

On the trip back to David's, I asked to learn more about the contracts and their marketing. David invited me to witness him in an actual presentation.

We arrived at David's house and went inside. Edith was all smiles and was even more convincing than her husband. She was really sold on the president, Mr. Steed, and the company.

"I had told David that if he ever went back into the insurance business, I would divorce him! He'll tell you how I burned everything in the house that had the name of Golden State, the first insurance company he was with. It just ruined us financially."

She showed me all of the jewelry that had been won by them for the week. David went through the Great National presentation. It was impressive. I was so caught up in what was going on, I forgot that my wife had been waiting for me and I had not called her, and so I told David and Edith I needed to go home.

"I will call Helen and smooth it over," Edith confirmed.

David invited me to attend the next Saturday's meeting.

Now I had all the information I needed, and because I respected David and Brad, I decided I would go with the company.

There was still a selling job to convince Helen. By the time I arrived home, supper had been served and the children had missed their ride. Helen was stewing. I had broken a promise. She was lying on the bed after having tucked the boys into their beds. She did not speak.

I went right to work to convince her on what a good opportunity this was. I shared all of the information I had learned.

"Helen, I believe I have finally found a position that will afford us all that we have ever wanted or could ever desire. David is now working in a position that white men have had for years, and we are lucky that there is a man, a good man, who wants Black men to have the same opportunity. I am asking you to go along with me to a meeting, and then I want you to help me with this decision. I do not believe that I will ever have to change jobs again. As convincing as David, Edith, and Brad were, I feel this is my last job.

"First, before you say anything to me, I want to apologize for not coming back for lunch or dinner. And secondly, I want you to call Edith and talk to her about the whole thing, then I want you to—"

The phone rang. It was Edith, and, as Helen answered it, Edith started right in on her, selling and selling. Edith must have said all the right things; after her phone conversation, Helen seemed very open to the idea of my changing jobs and began to talk seriously about the company and the impending changes in our lives if I took advantage of this opportunity.

David had assured me that the bonuses were to help a man break into the business until he delivered his contracts. Helen and I discussed how we would fair if things did not work out.

She had faith that I would succeed in anything I was given an opportunity to accomplish.

The next week did not go by fast enough. On Friday, before the meeting, Helen and I had made our decision, and we took out one of the contracts with David because, as he had convinced me, it would be good to show my total belief in the company and my sincere desire to become a part of it all.

It was Saturday. Helen and I rode to the meeting with Brad and his wife, Marla. We had breakfast in the coffee shop of the Dallas Marriott Hotel, where all the meetings were to be held. It was late October and near Halloween.

The company staff had decorated the entire banquet room in Halloween décor, as they would on each succeeding Saturday in decors of Election 1968, Thanksgiving, and the holiday season, along with Southwest Conference football. The time before the meeting was filled with an air of excitement and prosperity. People were outgoing and friendly, and everyone greeted associates and prospective associates enthusiastically. It was sort of funny to see men coming to the meeting in white cowboy hats and driving Cadillacs.

David introduced us to Mr. Steed as the greatest sales team the company would ever employ. The famous president's face blushed with a cheery redness, and his smile seemed honest. On the surface, he appeared to be all that had been said about him. The meeting began with prayer. There was singing and religion and an attitude of warmth flowed from person to person. The dais was occupied by region managers, the agency director, training instructors, and Mr. Steed. They sat on an elevated stage facing the crowd of associates, district managers, visitors, commanders, and their wives. Helen and I had been encouraged by Edith to dress our best. We did look the part and fit in with the stylishly dressed crowd of over two hundred.

Mr. Steed showered monetary gifts on associates for their accomplishments during the week. It appeared that they all looked forward to the next Saturday and more rewards. Mr. Steed looked the millionaire part, but his speech impediment added a different dimension to his story. We watched a movie about Steed's life and about the building of Great National. Then Mr. Steed spoke.

"Genesis 37:15 asked, 'What are you looking for?' The individual is blest who constantly pursues a quest. Its helps promote urge and ambition to better one's state or condition. It gives impetus to strive, to keep alert, keen, and alive. It makes for summits and high goals and lights a fire in men's souls. So always have a quest that you, with all your vigor can pursue."

I was impressed by his Christian beliefs and his ability to show it in testimony to this group. I decided I would be there in two weeks. In the interim, Brad and other associates had completed the training school and had won prizes at the following Saturday meeting.

First class was not the word for the style of meeting this company put on for its employees. Extravagant would better fit its description.

I had to raise $184 for tuition to pay the company to attend the training school. This created a problem for me, because I had just created costly medical bills because of my recent examinations and a tremendous loss due to expenses and illness on my current job.

David volunteered to pay it because the bonus system provided for a two hundred-dollar bonus to David for hiring me. I also had an opportunity to earn a two hundred-dollar bonus for placing five contracts after I was licensed. The company also offered one hundred dollars for five contracts in a week, a Rolex watch for ten contracts in a week, and one thousand dollars for twenty contracts in a thirty-day period. In addition, there could be weekly surprise bonuses of much greater worth.

I entered the training school. I had already memorized the presentation, so the school was a breeze. I spent most of my time helping the other prospects learn their presentation. Reading the presentation to a client did not convince them that you knew what you were presenting. The school changed my outlook on life because there was much religious emphasis placed in the work. It was as though the instructors were teaching preachers who knew all about the insurance industry and the art of selling, or, as Great National preferred, placing the contracts.

For the moment, I had forgotten about my physical condition. It was not apparent to others, and so there was no need to worry that the company would find out and thereby ruin my plans to utilize this opportunity to secure my family's future. I had to convert my health insurance because this company did not provide benefits. Associates were contract agents and responsible for their own benefits and taxes. Now all I thought about was making money. When I would make the money promised and laid out in the promotional packages, I would not have to worry about benefits. I would not let my illness slow me down. In effect, I had stopped feeling sorry for myself.

On Friday morning, graduation day, our class travelled to the home office of Great National, where the company holds a devotional service every Friday morning for the school's graduates and the staff. On occasion, they would have someone of importance who demonstrated a work life focused on Christian principles to be a guest speaker.

Often, the company would have a motivational speaker to encourage the new associates to start to build a sound future with Great National. This experience topped everything that David had said about the company. To me, here was a company practicing Christianity in its workplace.

It was a requirement that all clerical and office staff attend so they could give thanks for their opportunity and for the handling of the week's production by its sales force.

The next week was frustrating and heartbreaking for Helen and me. I could not begin working until I had received the insurance license. I was at the door each day waiting for the postman to bring my letter of confirmation to no avail.

Helen did everything possible to calm me, because

she knew that I did not understand the reason for the delay after David had promised that I would have my insurance license after finishing school. I had passed the examination, and my application had been processed before I entered the school. I practiced the presentation on friends. I was assured that I knew all about making the sale when I had convinced three of my friends to make the investment. The secret was in memorizing the presentation and then making it into a conversation, which appeared to show my complete knowledge about the program. I felt miserable because I could not complete an application unless I was licensed. I was reassured by my efforts. Through the practice, I had become an effective salesman, confident that the license was all I needed to begin achieving my goal.

It was now into late November, and the staff had decorated the meeting room in the décor of Thanksgiving. The usual greeting of new associates and prospects prevailed. There was a special aura about this meeting. The president and the managers were aloof, and, while keeping to themselves, there was still a feeling in the air that this would be another fantastic and rewarding meeting. At roll call, I had to report "no license."

This meeting proved more reassuring than ever. Mr. Steed offered a bonus for fifteen contracts placed that week of twenty-five thousand dollars and poured the cash out of a briefcase from the dais onto the floor. No one had qualified. I felt I could have easily qualified if only I had received the license. David was the highest producer, and the seemingly generous Mr. Steed gave him $1600 for his hiring of associates.

After arriving home, the postman brought the license certificate. I continued the work of searching for a commander. A commander, who was respected for his business judgment, was that center of influence. He would know many clients and friends who would qualify for investing in a contract. I found such a man in Ronald DeWitt, a school principal and entrepreneur in real estate ventures. Mr. DeWitt was busy all the time, and it was hard for me to tie him down to complete his commander's application.

At first, DeWitt was only interested in having me help him get an interview with Mr. Steed for a possible investment of Great National in his real estate endeavors.

I would eventually assist him in obtaining financing for his projects through other contacts with a different insurance company. He helped me with referrals, and through sales presentations I was able to place ten contracts in my first week after being licensed.

Helen was all smiles on the next Saturday morning. The expectation of the bonuses and the recognition, which would come, left only good feelings.

On more than one occasion while making the presentation to a client, my nose would visibly start bleeding. I was not sure whether the clients felt sorry for me, causing them to accept what I was selling, or whether I was doing a great job of presenting. Many of them would rush to grab tissues to assist me in stopping the bleeding. I could not tell them the reason why I had this condition. Still I was able to close each presentation and entice the clients to take advantage of the Great National program.

I was the top producer for that week, and all my associate friends thought I would walk off with the same bonuses that an associate, Luther Johnson, had the week prior when he received two thousand dollars in bonuses for placing ten contracts.

At the meeting that week, it was announced that the bonuses were cut. *Could it have been changed because management knew on Friday how many contracts I had placed?* That was all I could think; however, no associate inspired by Mr. Steed would even go there. I only received a Rolex watch and $250 for my production in addition to a pair of Justin alligator shoes and a Resistol white Stetson hat. I still had time to qualify for twenty contracts in less than thirty days.

Therefore, the next week proved that I worked hard to meet the goal and was excited when I exceeded my objective. I placed ten more contracts and was top man again. The staff at the company said a check accompanying one of my contracts had been misplaced, and I did not win the thousand-dollar bonus for twenty. I was awarded a camera set, a stereo, and another Rolex watch. At this meeting, I was given my first chance to talk to the group assembled in form of a testimonial.

In the Great National tradition, I gave tribute to Mr. DeWitt.

"I could not have achieved this production without the assistance of my commander, Ronald DeWitt."

I called him to the podium. "Mr. DeWitt, would you come up here with me? This is where you belong."

The associates and managers on the dais gave DeWitt a standing ovation as he walked to stand beside me at the microphone.

I gave him the Rolex watch. In an emotional exchange, DeWitt removed his old watch, threw it on the floor, and received another ovation.

Speaking was another talent that came easy to me and to the surprise of the assembly. My testimonial proved that, indeed, I was a professional and one who was moved by a belief in God.

The company cancelled all meetings until after the Christmas holidays, but that did not stop me from selling. I went out and sold twelve more contracts the next week. I became the first Black man of the month. The name of Richard Martin buzzed throughout the entire company and in all of its thirty-eight states of operation. My contracts started paying off.

I had sold over $1 million in insurance protection on the thirty-two contracts in the month of December 1968. I was disappointed that there were no weekly awards meetings and I did not receive the awards that others had for even less of an accomplishment, so I planned to achieve the same production in the first month of the New Year.

The annual company convention was near, and with Helen pregnant and having similar medical problems that had resulted in two miscarriages in the same year. I really worried about her. I had a friend whose wife died after three close miscarriages, and with this thought, I began feeling sorry for myself. It was a reminder of my problem and the secret visits to the doctor. My production fell off for the next two weeks. I wanted to tell Helen what was happening with me; however, because I was worried about her condition, I decided to wait until after her problems were over. I did not want her to give up and endanger her health because of the knowledge that I might die.

One other requirement that Mr. Steed imposed on his associates was that they have a financial obligation of some kind in order to give them an incentive to get up, get out, and see the people. Owning a new home and a new Cadillac were the biggest obligations of all. John Hooper had been promoted to agency director and David to a position titled assistant to the agency director. David had been pressing the associates to purchase Cadillacs. However, I could not because I needed the money for more important matters.

Brad Morgan, now my district manager, had purchased his car. David arranged with Brad to sell his car to me and purchase another. A South Oak Cliff Bank banker who was a former tight end for the Dallas Cowboys and a member of the NAMD made the transaction happen. That made down payments nil, and little did I know that arrangements had been made for a ninety-day payoff. David kept preaching that everyone would be able to pay off the cars in ninety days.

As keyed up as Mr. Steed and Great National had everyone, there could be no doubt that the cars would be paid off because of the rate at which sales were progressing. John Hooper, the agency director, had just paid his car off in less than ninety days. Although I had earned $11,085 in the month of December, I had not delivered all of my contracts. Besides, each contract paid income that would be received over a ten-year period, providing that the contract owners kept up their contracts.

The pride of ownership for a twenty-seven-year-old was important to me, and I soon began to accept the obligation and utilized the effect of the Cadillacs on my clients. Mr. Steed had a good plan with charging his associates to wear Louie Roth suits, alligator shoes, Rolex watches, and other expensive apparel, as it overwhelmed most of my customers into a conviction that I was a successful young man.

January was the month for the big gala affair at the Statler Hilton Hotel. Mr. Steed had arranged for guest speaker, Napoleon Hill, a famous motivational author of *Think and Grow Rich*, a required reading for all new associates. He gave a presentation on "How to Get Mink Coats and Cadillacs." Marilyn Van Derbur spoke on "Goals and Dreams." Reverend Billy G. Rivers gave the devotional. Chester Lauck, the extemporaneous salesman/comedian, made the associates laugh and cry. Many other big-name artists and authors were hosting the seminars. He had told everyone that the convention cost would be over fifty thousand dollars for the two-day event. All of the employees were treated like kings and queens. The main ballroom held over five hundred guests. The ballroom was decorated to give the feel of being in Hawaii. There were Hawaiian waiters and waitresses dressed in grass skirts and adorned with beautiful flowers. Six muscular Hawaiian men carried the main course of roast pigs on their shoulders up and down the rows between our tables. They stopped in front of the dais, and Ronald Steed blessed the meal.

This was the month following the "Man of the Month" award, which I had earned. The entire company had been notified. Maybe it was because I was the last man of the month prior to the convention that caused everyone to want to meet me and offer congratulations. From thirty-eight states, they came and all were aware of my accomplishments. There were only a few insurance salespeople who had sold a million dollars of individual life insurance in one year, let alone in one month.

Helen became sick on the second day, and I had to leave the convention to take her to the hospital. On the way, she talked about meeting with Dwayne Bowles, who had come to the convention to present a portrait to Mr. Steed. Bowles, as we found out later, was going to be regional manager in California.

Sadly, Helen miscarried again but made it through her treatment, and, in the end, my fears for her health were unfounded. After we took her home to recover, I went back to work.

There were no meetings until the first of February. I still had not received full recognition from the company for my efforts in December. I had qualified for all bonuses, but there was no indication that bonuses would be given. I was disheartened because I had not received the types of bonuses that others had for less achievement.

It was about one week before the first-of-the-month meeting, and David was hurriedly preparing to leave for the home office when he told Edith, "The Company is going to do something for Richard Martin for his production in December. We know he needs it to produce as he did in December."

"Why didn't he get the money for what he sold? I thought he qualified, and I know Helen feels bad about the lack of recognition that Richard has had from the company," Edith said.

"I can't answer that now," replied David. "But I don't think it will be money either."

"Why don't you just call Helen and build her up, but don't mention the prize. Oh! Mr. Steed wants you to meet him for lunch; I think he wants to talk to you about us buying a fifty thousand-dollar house. Meet him at noon at Neiman's. I'm on my way to the managers meeting, and I'll find out what they are going to do for Richard."

Edith hurried to finish her house cleaning to get ready for the luncheon with Mr. Steed.

David arrived at Great National building for the meeting, and all the managers were there, including Dwayne Bowles. John Hooper stated that he had a standing offer when he was region manager to anyone who produced thirty contracts in one month an award of the prized starburst tie tack. Only Dan Ratcliffe of West Virginia had qualified, although Mr. Steed, his son, A. J. Steed, Hooper, David, and the new region manager, Will Whitman, who also came from Humble Oil, each owned one. Hooper charged Whitman to uphold the offer.

"Will, I feel that you kinda owe that to Richard Martin since you were the region manager in December."

"Do you realize how much money you are talking about, John?" replied Will. "I know the man has done a good job, but I don't think that he is that good. We are talking about $1,500 for that diamond pin!"

They started to take a vote among the managers, but then Mr. Steed broke in and demanded that he purchase the pin. He was demanding and firm in his office with managers.

"But Mr. Steed, I won't have it ready for the meeting," Will exclaimed.

A. J. Steed, his son, and the agency superintendent interjected.

"Will, you can present him with my pin, and when his is ready, I'll take it, and that will solve your problem."

Everyone agreed on that solution, and now David knew what Richard would be awarded.

Mr. Steed approached David after the meeting and asked if Edith was going to meet him for lunch.

"You bet. No problem. I think she is woman enough to talk to you about anything concerning me that you want. She knows how to handle herself."

"Fine," Steed barked. "I'm late now. I'll see you in the office at six in the morning." That meant David should be there at 5:50 a.m. Ten minutes early was considered Ronald Steed's time.

David felt that Mr. Steed would help him purchase an expensive home as he had helped others purchase theirs. Mr. Steed wanted his managers projecting success in every area.

Edith arrived before Mr. Steed and visited the powder room in Neiman's to make sure she looked her best. She met Steed, and he immediately took her upstairs and purchased a beautiful dress. Then he took her to lunch and broke the silence of the meal.

"Edith, you are a pretty colored girl, and you are 98 percent of David. He will not be anything without you and your help. I want to see that you never have anything to worry about for the rest of your life. If you walk with me and do all that I say, I will see to it that you never suffer again. If anything happens to David, you will not have to be concerned for yourself and your children. I have seen a lot of women stand in the way of their husband's success. I know you won't. You know that Ronald Steed is a fair man. I have millions, and I can help you become a millionaire. Ronald Steed needs a woman, because it is God's will that I can help you become rich and it is God's will that you do something for me. You have got a lot at stake. You need to have all of the wealth, pretty expensive dresses like the one I just bought for you, and more that I will buy you and make sure, starting tomorrow morning, that David will be able to buy for you. Just let me help you. It is also God's will that you help Ronald Steed. I need you, and I want you to come with me to my hotel."

After a brief silence, he continued.

"Are you surprised to find out that Ronald Steed is a man?"

"No," replied Edith quietly.

"What is your answer? Do you want to have everything your heart desires, or do you want to ruin your husband's life?"

"I certainly don't want to ruin my husband's life, but I will not jeopardize our marriage by going to bed with you. Nothing against you, Mr. Steed, but we respect you so much that an act like that will demolish all the beliefs we have in you and the company. I do not think you will personally obstruct David's chances for success, because if he leaves, so will all the other colored men, and the big investments they and the company have made will go down the drain. Let's just keep it the way it is for now. You don't have to worry. I'll keep this between you and me."

"Edith, that was a test, and you passed with flying colors," Steed announced.

"Wow. For a minute there, I thought you were seriously hitting on me," Edith responded with a sigh of relief and continued to think what would have happened had she agreed. *Was he really serious? Was this really a test?*

Before going home, Edith stopped by to talk to Helen. As their conversation became obsessed with talk about Ronald Steed, Edith said, "Girl, Ronald Steed, told me I won't have anything to ever worry about, so David had better walk the talk or—"

"Or what?" Helen questioned.

"Well, whether he stays with the company or not or if he dies, I won't have a thing to be worried about. Oh, and something special is going to happen to Richard, so stop worrying about the problem with December rewards."

Helen asked Edith about what she meant, but Edith could not give her any details because she had not talked to David. Helen was still worried about the awards, and the suspense was killing her.

I was attending a business meeting at Mr. DeWitt's home. DeWitt introduced me to a group of his business associates and offered me a position with his firm once they were in operation.

DeWitt often praised me to other people because of my accomplishments and often confided in me with the confidential nature of his business ventures and would frequently say, "Martin, you are right in the middle of this, and I'm going to put you on the board of my company."

DeWitt liked to boast about his business and was constantly bragging about his success, even though he was failing to obtain the interim financing for his shopping center projects. He had recently visited with Ronald Steed to offer him an opportunity to invest in a corporation designed to build major complexes in and around the city of Dallas. Mr. Steed was ready to invest until he talked with David, who downgraded DeWitt, causing Steed to change his view. David did not like other Black men going to Mr. Steed with a cause. It was almost as though he wanted the exclusive.

Upon my arrival home, Helen told me about the conversation with Edith. Now I worried about what would happen. I hoped I would receive the bonus money.

It was the Sunday morning before the regional meeting, and both Helen and I had woken up early because we could not sleep.

"You know what, Helen? It looks like it is going to take longer for us to reach the point that the money will be rolling in, but I was thinking back to what I have done best on this job and what I got the most satisfaction out of was when I hired the two men, and it was easy.

"I feel I should take off and go on a hiring spree to Louisiana. I could earn more money, and if I hired twenty-five men a month and wrote a contract on each one of them, I would make five thousand dollars for hiring at two hundred dollars per man and seven thousand dollars on the contracts, and there is no telling what Mr. Steed would do. I know that I can achieve that goal. In fact, I'm going to talk to David and Brad and let them know what I will do."

The phone rang, and Helen answered. It was David.

"Put Richard on the phone."

"What are you calling on a Sunday morning for? Don't you ever get away from Great National?" I asked.

"No, I was thinking about you, and I wanted to tell you about something that is going to happen to you."

I nudged Helen, and she snuggled up to the phone to hear. He continued. "How would you like to go to California as a district manager?"

I was shocked, but Helen grabbed the phone and said, "California! March first is when we will be ready to go."

Taking the phone back, I affirmed. "That's right, March first. God has answered our prayers, the reason we answered the phone so quick was because we were talking about my going to another state to hire men, but little did I know you would call and give the answer."

"That's amazing," David remarked. "I have talked to Mr. Steed, and he agreed to walk with you. He will setup a twenty-five thousand-dollar bank account that Dwayne Bowles, the new state manager, will control for your operating expenses, and I will also go with you to help you get started."

"Will the company pay for our move?" Helen asked.

"No. Look, the best thing for you is to sell all of your furniture and get enough money to move Helen and the boys back to your hometown."

"I will have to think about that. Why can't the company pay?" I asked.

David hedged. "Once you get settled, and if you need some money, I will talk to the old man, but I don't want to go with a weak case before we get there, so think about selling your furniture and paying off your bills and you can get a new start in California. The cost to store and move the furniture will be more than it would take to replace it over there, and you probably wouldn't be able to pay off your bills."

I told David that we would come by after Mass and give him an answer one way or the other. Bills were mounting up again on us, and I dearly wanted to go to California because I could pursue my hiring dream. Helen and I talked about selling the furniture and paying off bills to make the new start in California.

It was a decision we prayed on at the Mass. Father Joe had been away managing another parish since I had first indicated to him that there was a problem to discuss with him. Because I had missed the appointment and feared facing up to the priest with my problem, I asked Brad to lector in my place. I did not go to Holy Communion for the same reason, but Father Joe noticed me after Helen returned to the pew following Holy Communion.

I had begun to run away from my obligations. I had constantly put off paying for the Ford convertible in hopes that my contracts would pay off, enabling me to pay it off in full, but the credit union would soon repossess it and help me make up my mind about running off to California. The priest met me after Mass, and we talked in private for an hour. Helen had gone home and indicated she would return to pick me up. I forced myself to tell him about the cancer and the threat of death. I also told him all about the experiences with Great National. Father Joe advised me to make the change to California but could not understand why I had to sell all my furniture. Father Joe gave me his blessings and instructed me.

"You should have the Sacrament of the Infirm administered because you may not be near a priest when it happens."

I promised I would be in constant contact with my doctor, who had me taking four pure calcium tablets daily to balance my pH and acidity levels.

Afterwards, Helen and I gave David the decision to move to California. We would sell the furniture because we had faith in the company and in him and planned to make the transition on March first.

David had arranged for me to meet Dwayne Bowles. Bowles had been going back through the training school where David picked him up. They drove to my house where Helen had prepared dinner. The conversation was controlled by Bowles. He had wanted to meet "Richard Martin" to learn what made him tick. He supposedly was concerned about me being a twenty-seven-year-old manager. During the course of that evening, Bowles laid out his plans for California and his region. His goals were conservative to those of mine, the big thinker. I had plans of becoming a millionaire in two years. My goal was realistic and all based on hiring the right kind of associates and the right growth number of men.

I had written a letter to Ronald Steed with my own goals when I shared the information with Bowles. He realized that he was not going to be working with an ordinary salesman. I demonstrated my drive and ambition, and it was backed up with sound fiscal projections.

I felt I would enjoy working with Bowles, who was an accomplished insurance actuary. The regional meeting was one of the largest single gatherings of all five states' personnel. As the meeting progressed, Ronald Steed called me up to the podium and presented me with the tie tack. In a display of my surprise and feeling of accomplishment, I removed my old ten-dollar tie tack, threw it on the floor, and replaced it with the prize.

It would have been nice to have received money, but this was an award with which only a few had been honored; one that would last forever. My promotion was announced, and it was a big surprise to the gathering. They gave me a standing ovation. I was so moved by the outburst of well wishes that I shed a few tears of happiness, and then I spoke to the meeting attendees.

In my speech, I accepted the challenge to do something great in California, and I offered a challenge to the meeting attendees.

Ronald Steed interrupted my speech to share that I had already made a commitment to help make California the number one producing state.

As I concluded my comments, I challenged the regional state delegations to continue their work and to watch for me in the *Bellringer*, a weekly newsletter that the company published that contained results of the prior week.

During the week that followed, I was asked to speak at two meetings. I assisted David in hiring three men in Austin, Houston, and Dallas.

I gained courage during that week to tackle the challenges that lay before me in California. I had become the number one booster of Great National and Ronald Steed.

In the last week of February, we were able to sell the last of the furniture, and Helen and the children traveled to her mother's while I stayed with David. We planned to leave in two days.

The trip to California was an experience. I had never been out West, and when we ran into snow in New Mexico and northern Arizona, I wished I had taken the plane. However, this trip gave David and me an opportunity to learn about each other and to plan the calls we would initially make on arrival. We had formulated a list of important individuals to set up as commanders and for the hiring of associates. David recalled, as we were traveling, the experience he had with Brad Morgan and his wife before they left.

"Brad had wanted to go to California, but I knew that you were the best man for the job. I often told Edith that you were the best man I had hired, even after coming out of school and before you started producing. I knew you were a self-starter, and that is why I didn't help you or why you didn't have anyone to train you after being licensed."

"Is that so?" I remarked. "I thought you didn't have time for me. I really thought that everyone left me alone and had no confidence that I would make it. In fact, no one really started fraternizing with me until I was top man."

David assured me that the only reason I was not given the training afforded to others was because I was better than any of the other associates.

"And you proved that in December."

I still contended that if I had had assistance, I could have produced even more, because there were many applications lost because I did not have the sales closing skills to secure the sale. David agreed, but only to an extent.

It took us two days and a night to arrive in California. We stopped in Albuquerque to visit with a new associate, Russell Stafford, who would later join me in California. We gave him information and some training on setting up a commander. We arrived in Compton, California, around eight o'clock and stopped at David's sister's home. We would stay there until I found a furnished home or an apartment for my family.

Nellie Green was almost a facsimile of David. She was a muscular and heavy woman, mainly because of her position as high school swimming instructor. She had the shrewdness of her brother, and it showed in her domineering relation with her quiet schoolteacher husband. They welcomed me into their home. David had cautioned me not to make jokes about her weight because she was easily hurt. However, he had also noted that I should listen to them about their experience in California and their insight about how to relate to people in California. Nellie pried into the type of business we were involved in and gave her advice on men in California.

"These people are different out here, and you won't find it as easy as it was back in Texas. They are basically cold toward anybody new to them. They have had confidence games run on them so much that it keeps them from getting involved in something from another state. Whatever it is you are selling, it is going to take time to get started. About ninety days and you will have it made."

"So, listen to us when we tell you about calling on the people here," her husband added.

"See what I mean." David broke in. "My sister and her husband, because they have been through the mill in California, know what they are talking about."

"The California Negro and also the white man are different from all people," she continued.

I was moved by their dissertation on the transplanted Californian. I was easily impressed by the Greens and with the people they knew. Especially when they took me over to their friend's house and I placed my first California contract. I began to formulate an opinion that it would not be easy and this might fail, even in future sales presentation. I might give up without trying to close, failing on the pretense that this was yet another cold Californian. For the moment, I was reassured by this first sale.

I set up Mr. Green as a commander. I had not been able to close any contracts from the new prospects I had been given and really believed all they had told me about the different attitudes of the Californian people. A month had passed and I had set up a dentist, some prominent businessmen, and a minister as commanders for the new associates I was going to hire.

I would have to find a place to live that was close to Dwayne Bowles, thereby making it convenient for us to meet every morning to formulate plans for building the state and the region.

David had to go back to Texas. Brad Morgan had called and informed him that he was quitting.

"I don't feel that everything is right about this company, and I have a need to make some money, so I'm going to get a salary job," was Brad's statement.

David was so frustrated because he could not change Brad's mind on the telephone. David called Texas to find out from the company and from John Hooper exactly what had to be done. He felt that if Brad quit, others would follow. David had gotten permission to offer Brad one thousand dollars per month plus twenty dollars per contract that was written in his district, but Brad passed that up, and I began to worry.

Knowing Brad, he would not turn down an offer like that unless something drastic had happened. I told David that if Brad quit, I'd find out why, and if it was strong enough, I would quit too.

David became more worried and left his sister's home to phone Bowles from a pay phone. Their conversation was about Brad and his reason for quitting. Brad had told David, but he would not reveal it to me.

David set up a meeting place with Bowles to talk me into staying. Sometime later, when I would visit with Brad, I learned that he phoned Brad and pleaded with him to make sure he kept his word and never told me his reasons for ending his career. Later that night, David and I met Bowles at a coffee shop in Los Angeles. When we walked in, Bowles was sitting at a table.

They were able to impress me with their promises, and they said that Brad was quitting because he was not a very strong individual and could not work on commissions. David again praised me as being the best that was hired. Although convinced enough to continue, I felt that all was not right.

The subject of the conversation changed to David's trip back to Texas. In the middle of our discussion, a group of Black men walked into the coffee shop. They looked like Great National men in every respect, except the fedoras they wore were not like the white Stetsons worn by the three of us. Eyes were on us, piercing with what appeared to be concern for their turf. David discerned that they were pimps, and this was verified as several ladies of the night walked into the coffee shop and handed money to them.

This was a spot for the pimps to meet and make their collections. They must have thought we were moving in on their territory. One of the pimps walked over to our table and started to eyeball our tie tacks and jewelry. He wanted to start a conversation with us and to compare walking worth. All four of them were wearing expensive suits and alligator shoes, but the National men's jewelry was far better than the pimps.

The pimp offered to buy the diamond ring that Dwayne was wearing. It suddenly hit all three of us that one of their main problems could be that we reminded our customers and clients of these pimps, mainly because of our attire and the Cadillacs.

Dwayne became frightened as David brushed off the pimp. Dwayne, David, and I started out of the coffee shop. As we went to the Cadillacs outside, we planned to meet at Bowles' apartment but would split up and go in different directions. Two of the pimps had followed us outside, saw us by the Cadillacs, and ran back inside, shouting.

"They are for real. They are driving hogs too." Hearing this, we got into our cars and sped away as some of the pimps followed. We were able to lose them in the Los Angeles traffic on Manchester Boulevard and met later at Bowles' apartment in Playa del Rey.

The discussion that followed caused us to consider changing our image by dropping most of the jewelry and not wearing white hats except during recruiting. David returned to Texas to relay all that had occurred. This change proved successful as I went on the next week to produce five contracts and became Bellringer of the Week. The experience had also erased the thoughts that had concerned me about Brad Morgan quitting.

Bowles and I placed ads in the *Los Angeles Times*. They were of the type that invited hundreds of responses. With letters coming in for appointments and interviews, we set up in two adjoining rooms at the International Hotel near LAX. In the first two days of interviews, I had hired six associates.

Bowles, in the next room, had promised everyone he had interviewed that he would make them district manager soon after completing school. He used the portfolio on my "man of the month" accomplishments to convince his applicants to join the company. During a downtime from interviewing, I overheard his conversation through the adjoining door. Bowles would tell the white applicants, "If a Black man could accomplish that feat in Texas with Black folk, just think of what you could do with the California white customers."

However, he would also tell them that the man was in the next room and he would give them an opportunity to meet him. I would then utilize my talents to further convince them of the Great National way of life and sell them on Mr. Steed. I was able to accomplish this with all of the applicants he interviewed. However, Bowles needed assistance, and *he was the regional manager*.

Bowles hired four men that week. I learned later how he begged them to come to the company and made commitments to them. When they went to Dallas to attend the school, they learned that all was not the same as described by Bowles, and so they quit and returned to California. One of them had called me to wish me success and to explain how Bowles conducted his interview. I was thoroughly convinced of the company's way of doing business and did not fully understand what was going on. I believed that Ronald Steed was second to God and felt close to him. My belief in Steed's philosophy of life and his concept of sharing with others was foremost in my mind. I preferred to project the qualities I admired in Ronald Steed as a leader to get new recruits into the business rather than promising financial incentives. I knew I was not alone in my feeling and convictions about Mr. Steed. Many associates grew, quickly, to feel the same way.

The men I hired came because they believed the stories I told about Mr. Steed and wanted to work for a man of that stature. There was probably no man more dedicated to the company and Steed than I. There was the time at the January convention that Steed showed concern about Helen going to the hospital and told me, "I will make you a millionaire if you let me help you."

I never forgot that moment.

I sent for Helen and the boys after that week of hiring. I had been told I could rent a house that was vacant in Playa del Rey. The property owner changed his mind after he found out I was Black and raised the rent beyond what I could afford.

I had found it rough going in finding a place to live with children. Besides, the rent was three times as high as that in Texas. The home I was going to rent was $350 a month and was not nearly comparable to the one hundred-dollar home in Dallas. When my family arrived, I put them up in a hotel for a week while we tried to rent other homes.

Bowles and I had gone to call on one of the businesspersons who had become a commander with the company, and Bowles asked him to help me find a place to stay. He gave him the name of a woman who would have a place to rent in exclusive View Park neighborhood in one week. I called her and she told me I could have it. My housing problems were solved. Bowles had told me to take it no matter what the cost so that I could concentrate on my production. I moved my family out of the hotel and back with the Greens. They had asked me to stay there until the house was vacant.

Helen and I had not talked much since she arrived, and we had our first confrontation. Right after they had arrived, I had asked my eldest son about the people he met in Texas. My son told me about the people he met and mentioned the name of one of his mother's high school boyfriends. I asked for trouble when I questioned him further, and he added that his mother had gone into a bedroom at her sister's house with this man and he could hear noises that sounded like the time he walked in on us together. This shocked me coming from my son. The boy had always possessed an excellent memory and always told me the truth. Helen was in the kitchen talking to Nellie. I sent my son in with a note that read, "Richard Jr. told me about Jack. Come here. I want to talk to you."

Helen was afraid of what I would do and did not come to talk to me. Instead, she talked to Nellie and told her that I was angry.

"I don't know what Richard Jr. told him, but I'm not going in there because if he's angry, he may beat me up."

Nellie advised her to overpower me and act like she did not know what I wanted to talk about.

"Walk in there with your chest out and question him about what he's been doing since he has been here," Nellie said. "And put him on the defensive, whether it's true or not. Is it true?"

"I don't really know what Jr. told him, but he probably thinks I was running around with that man."

"What you ought to do," Nellie advised, "is beat up Richard Jr., because if my son ever told anything on me, I would tear his little butt up."

They continued talking, but I was waiting patiently for her in the bedroom. Nellie came into the bedroom.

"Richard, what is wrong with you? You've got that poor girl crying her heart out."

"Did she send you in here to do her talking?"

"No. She is scared that you will knock her head off. How could you believe what that little boy told you? Don't you have any faith in your wife? Don't you trust her?" Nellie asked.

"Not now," I replied. "First of all, I just asked her to come in here to talk to me. If she had come immediately, I would have known that Richard Jr. could have been mistaken about what went on, and I would have whipped him. But she didn't come, and to me that is an admission of guilt. And secondly, you do not know her as I do. If she made a mistake, she should be woman enough to try and lie out of the situation, but she has only proven to me that I should not trust her or have any faith in her. And lastly, I don't want to talk to you about it. She is the one who has to answer to me and not you for her."

"I am a woman," Nellie answered abruptly, "and whether you believe it or not, I know another woman better than anyone. And I've talked to Helen, and the only reason she won't come is because she doesn't know what you will do to her. And if she did something or not, you don't really know and what you have not seen nor have knowledge of can't hurt you."

"Yes, but what you don't know about me is that I will never harm her or any woman."

I refused to talk anymore; however, Nellie went on.

"I've been in hot water before. So has my husband and so has David. But even I had to help him on one occasion. He was running around with another woman and when I found out from Edith, I went looking for him, and I found him in a nightclub sitting at a table with that other woman. I walked over to the table, took her beer bottle, raised it in the air, and told him to get his behind home to Edith or I would kill the both of them. Then I grabbed that woman and ushered her out of the door. David went home, and from that day forth I have not heard about him mistreating Edith. So you really don't know what went on, but give her a chance to tell you the truth or tell you a lie."

I was exhausted from all the emotions I was feeling and tired from working so hard to get my family together. I ended up falling asleep after Nellie left the room. Around 2 a.m., Helen came in the room. I was certain that my son had told the truth and that she was guilty, but I did not confront her and hoped that she would talk to me about it. I had too much to lose by pursuing this any further. I decided to move back to the hotel.

David was on his way back to California. He was driving out and on the way would pick up Russell in Albuquerque to come and help me continue to build California.

Back in Dallas, the man who started it all for David and everyone who followed, John Hooper, had resigned as agency director. I would not find out until David arrived. However, John had gone to his bankers to secure a loan on his home, and when they found out that he worked for Great National and Ronald Steed, they turned him down. John was not the kind of man who would let this pass so easily, so he acted on the advice of the bankers to check out the company and Ronald Steed's character with other bankers and insurance executives in the city. John was able to find out that Steed was considered a sick man, that he had a shrewd mind for making money. Steed was sick to the extent that he used the wives of employees and the women in his office in an attempt to satisfy his ego. John had secured information from women who had been approached by Steed. He took the information and his reports and confronted Steed with the evidence. Steed's reply was simply, "Boy, you can take that junk anywhere you want to, but I can buy off all your friends and anyone that you have on that there list."

John turned in his resignation and shocked Steed. He had hired many men, and they would follow in his footsteps. Steed knew this and attempted to offer Hooper a way out. Steed held the first mortgage on the house Hooper lived in and used this to threaten him. Steed also used the company account charged to the agency director in the amount of sixty thousand dollars that would have been cleared with his 1 percent override on all contracts produced in the company. However, if he resigned, he could receive no override, and the charges for meetings and gifts would still be there.

John knew that Steed had approved some advances and monthly draws over his signature, which was 90 percent of that account total, and he knew that one particular man in Virginia had come back to the company and bribed Steed into giving him twenty thousand dollars, which was charged to Hooper's account after the man quit.

John resigned and obtained an attorney to represent him in a suit against Steed. The lawyer was Jonathan McVea, who had quit just one month prior as company attorney after he had learned of Steed's moral background.

David arrived in California and met with Bowles. He told him about John Hooper and about what he was going to do to Steed. He had spent two nights with John and his wife, along with Edith, trying to work out the situation. John would not return and advised David to follow his lead or else be hurt as he was.

David told Bowles, "He could have all the money he wants if he would stay with the company. I guess he is just hardheaded. I am going to stay and drain as much as I can out of the old man, as you have advised me. The only person I am worried about, Dwayne, is Richard Martin. I wonder what he will do when he finds out. If he ever does find out about the old man, he could ruin your whole operation here in California, since he has hired most of your thirty-two men."

"I am not worried," replied Bowles. "I know he needs money right now, and since he is so stubborn and won't ask for it, I will wait until the last minute and get him an advance. I know that when he feels obligated to someone, he listens and follows whatever they tell him, especially if he is made to believe the instructions come from Mr. Steed. I can handle Richard Martin."

And Bowles did, because I did need money to pay bills, to move into the house, to buy furniture and food, and to operate. I had received no overrides from the contracts placed by the new men I had hired in California.

Bowles saw that I never got the money because he demoted me back to an associate. His reason was that I could not project the image of a manager because of my financial condition.

I was dejected but felt I would overcome this setback and become a top producer. I really felt things would turn around because the day before, I had set up a good commander, Foster Price, a real estate broker who, together with his wife, had invited me into their home. Mr. Price opened my eyes to the fact that people in California were not any different than the people back home. Mr. Price explained the Californian as being a person who has migrated to this state and expected the Californians to welcome him with open arms, only to find out that there were few true Californians, and that most people had migrated themselves and expected the same, so everybody is waiting for the next guy to make the first move toward becoming friends.

"And that's why they say people are cold and protective in California. They aren't really. All you have to do is to show a little kindness and people will welcome them in, just as we have you."

I respected this man. I thought back to nearly three months ago and the statements of David and the Greens and started to understand why I had not closed most of my presentations. How wrong they had been. In my heart, I accepted the demotion that gave me freedom to work for myself alone. I had turned over supervisory responsibilities to two new white district managers.

On my first call to prospects recommended by Mr. Price, I placed three contracts with a dentist. I handled the presentations just as I did back in Texas in December, including the sympathetic nose bleeding, which I could not control because of my condition.

I moved my family into the unfurnished house. I picked up the personal goods we had shipped and stored at one of Helen's aunt's home. My family had to sleep on borrowed mattresses on the floor. I shopped at many stores and could not obtain credit because of my newness to California and my commission-based job.

No one in the whole company knew just how much my family was sacrificing in order for me to work for Great National. Helen withstood this sacrifice better than I had expected because she had never been exposed to this type of poverty. Without money, I could not continue to produce, and with my family living from day to day, I began to consider whether or not I had made the right decision to sell our furniture and come to California without help from the company, and I wondered why my family should have to go through this ordeal.

Helen had called her grandfather, who had raised her from a baby, and tried to get him to help. He did not want to help because he was a cold and callous old man who had the Midas touch with money but had the heart of an unreformed Ebenezer Scrooge. She was disheartened by the decision, and for the first time since I had joined the company, she wanted me to quit. She felt that no one in the company would help as David had promised when he talked us into going to California and selling our furniture to get a new start.

For the first time in my life, I was willing to accept help from someone, anyone. I was known for having a strong sense of pride and wanting to be independent. Most people felt that I was hardheaded and wanted to be my own man, and that is what I had been, my own man. I had managed to provide for my family by being close to God. Helen recalled a time when I was waiting for my license at the beginning of this experience with the company, and there was no money coming in. I was on my knees night and morning in prayer. A check for back pay from the government that had been overlooked came in the mail and helped provide for food and shelter during that trying period, and the same type of miracle happened more than once.

I had five California contracts back in Texas, which had problems being approved because of medical reasons. These contracts finally came through, and I received money to help my family.

Time passed, and we learned to endure the hardship of sleeping on the mattresses on the floor. I still needed money to pay for the Cadillac and to be able to operate my business.

California had become the top-producing state, as I had promised, and I was the main contributor to the achievement both in the men I hired who had produced and in the personal production I had achieved.

Bowles had promoted two more white associates to district manager. I knew I could relieve my family of our financial situation by working on my production and becoming the state manager.

The associates in California, with their wives, were ordered to attend a seminar to be held in Dallas. Bowles had arranged for an advance for me, which I would receive upon my arrival in Dallas. Bowles had asked all associates to hold the contracts they had written until they went to Dallas. They would turn them in bulk and have the highest production for one week of any other state year to date.

The entire group flew to Dallas on a chartered Braniff Airlines jet in an expanded first-class section. We were met at Love Field by home office officials on our arrival in Dallas.

I renewed acquaintances with the people who remembered the Richard Martin of December. Individually, they recognized me for the job I had done in building California to a top-producing state. Steed met us at the hotel and congratulated me. I shook Steed's hand and tried to stay far away from him. I kept a safe distance by constantly knowing where Steed was. The plane ride had taken a lot out of me. I worried about my health. I would see Doctor Prince the next day. I could not bring myself to divulge my financial condition and of the sacrifices my family was enduring to Steed or my doctor friend.

The first meeting was held on the night that they arrived, and Steed offered five thousand dollars for any man who had produced fifteen contracts in the last two weeks. None qualified, as Steed knew beforehand. He had already talked with all the managers. That was his way of motivating them to sell. The meeting involved training sessions aimed at helping the associates place more business.

I met Edith in David's suite to discuss my situation in California and how I felt about the promises David and Mr. Steed made. David had not yet arrived.

"Edith, I know you probably don't know much about David's sister, but if it were not for her and your husband, my outlook toward the people in California would have been much better and perhaps I would not be in need of assistance today. They disillusioned me from the beginning and hurt me in my calls on the people there."

"I do know her," stated Edith. "And I warned David that it was not a good idea to stay there because I know the type of person she is. However, since he had you sell your furniture, he wanted to make it easier on you. I told him you should have gotten a small furnished apartment until Helen could come.

"She is something else," Edith continued as David walked in the door.

"Who's something else?" David questioned.

"Your sister is the person we have been talking about, but I realize that you have to go along with her because she is your blood, so let's not talk about her. We have more important things to discuss," I replied.

"Okay," David began. "How would you like to move back home? I have been talking to Bowles, and he wants you to stay in California, knowing that you have helped him get started, but we can use your talents back here."

I told David I had invested a lot of time and money with the men in California, even though I had not reaped the fruits of these investments. I wanted to remain in California because of the potential and because I loved all of the people I worked with and wanted to continue to help them build. If I came back to Texas, some of the men would fail.

"Did Bowles agree with you that I should come back to Texas?"

"He left it up to you, Richard. Since he demoted you, I don't believe you will ever be tops with him again. I don't believe you will be able to work with him anymore. I'll bet he makes one of the white guys the state manager."

"That'll be the day," I broke in. "There is not another man, white or Black, who is more qualified than me. After all, I have trained and inspired all of them, and I really believe when I start producing again, he will promote me."

"I believe you're wrong. I don't think he will put you over the white guys again, because you can't give the financial image you need to."

"Well, you know too well why I am in this shape. You know better than anyone else. I listened to you and sold my furniture. The company did not help me move

or reimburse me after I made the trip, which you promised to arrange. You messed up the minds of my men
when you came and scared them to death by telling
them how hard it was, because you had failed and could
not place business, and I feel that if these men were
given a chance to become self-starters, they would have
accomplished more than the record shows.

"Do you remember that I confronted you when you
tried to make me look bad in front of them? God says
I should forgive you for that. However, all of this, coupled with the information that I accepted from you and
your sister about the people in California, has made it
hard for me and is the reason my finances are in bad
shape. I guess that is what happens to a naïve man who
places his trust in the advice of another man, as I have
you. Needless to say, I want to go back to California,
and if I never receive a promotion, I will still be the best
associate this company ever had."

The heated discussion resulted in a mutual agreement on getting the company to help me. However, I
felt David was not telling all he knew. There was still
no truth forthcoming on Brad or John Hooper.

Helen and I talked about the conversation until the
early morning hours. We made decisions about the
company, and we decided that when we arrived back in
California, I could start to work on becoming the best
producer and that I would tell Bowles at some point during the meeting set for the next morning that I would
earn the right to be the state manager in one month.

Ronald Steed called for testimonials, which meant
that associates and managers would get up before the
group and confess how they felt about the company.

Helen had talked to Steed before the meeting began and related to him of the way our family had been living and the sacrifices we were all making. Steed had told her he would do something about the situation, and, seemingly, he was angry that neither Bowles nor David had told him.

Often, when testimonials were in session, I was one of the first to get up because I could really sell the company and Steed to anyone. Steed had witnessed me in action before and noticed I had not moved to get in line with others who wanted to testify.

He interrupted one of the men and stated, "There is a man in the group who is one of the strongest associates we have, and usually he has a lot on his heart to talk to us about, and I am wondering why he has kept quiet. That man is Richard Martin."

I stood up, and the group broke out with applause. Then I announced, "Mr. Steed, the podium is for winners, and normally I do not have anything to say unless I am a winner. I'm a loser at this meeting, but I may have something to say before this meeting is over."

I did not want to go before the group because some of the men had already testified and said some of the things I felt.

Steed continued, "That same young man has a wife who, if he lost her in a poker game, the winner would have to give her back, because she is so dedicated to him and his success. I want Mrs. Martin to come up right now and tell us what is on her heart."

Helen moved to the stage and gave a timely speech concerning a wife's involvement in her husband's work. She received an ovation, and Steed broke in and said,

"For that kind of belief in your husband and in the company, I am going to take you to Neiman Marcus and buy you one of the finest outfits you have ever seen."

Everyone applauded this award. Steed spoke again.

"Now you can come up, Richard Martin."

As I approached the head table, all of the associates and managers stood and gave me an ovation that lasted for two minutes. I had tears in my eyes as I began to speak.

Referring to Steed, I said, "This man is full of surprises. You never know what he's going to do next."

Little did I know what Steed had planned.

"I do have something to say, Mr. Steed, and even though I have the most production turned in at this meeting, I still consider myself a loser, mainly because I have not reached the goals I set before I went to California. I listened to the wrong people when I arrived in California, but I was able only recently to understand that people are the same no matter where you are, and that is why I will be the top associate or manager with this company. There is a spirit that surrounds everyone here that I call the Great National spirit. When you find a company that is concerned about an associate as if he were a member of its family, then you will have a company that is better than ours. I challenge each and every one of you to find yourselves with this company and catch on to this spirit. When you do, you will feel as I do about Mr. Steed and all of the people I know personally at Great National. I have grown to love each and every one of you, and if you feel like shedding tears like I am now, then do so, because you will have taken on the Great National spirit."

Steed took Helen to Neiman's. Although every woman wants to be able to shop at Neiman's, she was moved by the manner that Steed ordered people around in the store. John Wayne, the great actor, was in the store, and he became one of the spectators as Helen went through the ritual of modeling different dresses for the edification of Steed. He asked her, "Do you like that dress? Because I do, and I think you are real pretty in it."

Helen was overcome; this was ecstasy for her, the ultimate.

"Yes, sir," she answered. "But it is so expensive. I could buy twenty dresses for the cost of this one."

Steed told her not to worry about the cost because she deserved to have the best, and he would see to it that she did.

Steed noticed Helen's innocence and was pleased by her excitement. He knew he could really move her by buying her another dress. He picked one from the rack that cost $365, handed it to her, and said, "You deserve to have this one too."

Helen was really surprised and flattered by the attention. After the way we had been living in California, she felt like this was a dream of some kind. The saleswoman told her not to worry about anything because Mr. Steed really wanted to buy the dresses for her.

Helen thanked Mr. Steed and the saleswoman, and, as they left to go to lunch, Steed reassured the saleswoman Helen would be back.

"Her husband is a big man in California and he will be making lots of money," he said.

He had them deliver the dresses to her hotel room. As they walked down the street to eat lunch, Steed asked her if she would like me to be able to buy her dresses like that. She answered affirmative. He promised over lunch that he would talk to her about it.

At lunch, Steed began to use his lines that he had used in the past to make women feel obligated to please him.

"Helen, I noticed that you and Edith are always together. What is it between you two?"

"We are just good friends, Mr. Steed. We haven't seen each other for over five months, and we are just spending some time together."

"Does she tell much about her personal life and about David?"

"No, sir. Edith is not the kind of woman who talks about personal things with anyone, and she even told me that David doesn't know as much about the way she feels about certain things because she doesn't talk to him about women's personal things, and neither do I. A woman has to keep some secrets."

Helen really felt like someone special because Ronald Steed often bought gifts for other people, but he would always send his secretary or someone else to accompany them. Steed would rarely go to the stores. She felt honored that he was spending time with her personally and told him so.

Steed, sensing an opportunity, stated, "Helen, you are a beautiful young lady, and your husband is lucky to have you. He should be in a position to do great things for you. You need to have all of the wealth you deserve. A woman like you deserves to have dresses like I bought you, and if you help me help Richard, I will make him a millionaire. I have seen women stand in the way of their husband's success, but I know you will not.

I have got millions, and I am going to make it possible for you and your kids never to worry about anything. I will let you know how we will make Richard a millionaire. I will be in California in two weeks for your regional meeting. I want you to wear the party dress I just bought for you to the City Club of Dallas tonight. We are going to take everyone over there for a good meal. I want you to make me proud of you tonight."

Helen explained that she did not have the right shoes to wear with the dress, and Steed gave her a one hundred-dollar bill to buy shoes and a handbag.

This topped the entire day for her, and she looked around to see if any eyes were on them and kissed him on the cheek. She really loved the company now and knew I would be able to buy her nice things because Ronald Steed said so.

I had been busy with the business sessions of the seminar and had forgotten that Helen had gone shopping. I was reminded when I walked into my room to prepare for the big dinner. Helen had laid the dresses across the bed. They were beautiful and expensive.

"Over five hundred dollars' worth, baby," Helen sang.

She had told Steed about the experience and stated, "Mr. Steed took me to lunch and told me that he is going to help you get back on your feet and that if anything ever happened to you, the kids and I would not have anything to worry about."

"That's good. I knew something would come out of this trip. I am proud of the way you handled yourself at the meeting this morning, Helen. I really have a wife to be proud of. Lots of associates' wives said good things about you, and I just wanted to let you know that I am proud."

I felt I had finally made Steed notice me, and he would surely help us, just as he had helped David and others. We prepared for the dinner because I had to do some work on the presentation Bowles and I would give to the group that night.

When we arrived at the City Club of Dallas, where Steed was a member, I told him I wanted to talk. I wanted to thank Steed. As I stepped off the elevator, Steed called me aside. Steed was perspiring and seemed nervous, but as I spoke up, he seemed to calm down.

"I want to thank you for the dresses you gave Helen. I wish I were in a position to do the same. She feels proud that you have honored her, and I am indeed proud that you thought about us."

Steed replied calmly, "Richard, I'll make you a millionaire if you let me."

"That's one thing you don't have to worry about, sir. I am going to do great things for this company."

I was impressed once again with that millionaire statement and felt about ten feet tall. The presentation was a success as we discussed a booster's-type meeting that had produced some business in California. It was presented for use by those from other states.

On the final day, Steed invited everyone to a catfish fry and a jaunt around the lake on his yacht, which held over one hundred and fifty passengers.

The next morning, I called Mr. DeWitt, my former commander in Dallas. He had received the final financing through the contact I supplied him. All of his projects were in full swing. He offered me a position, but I refused. Great National was my life, and DeWitt could not help me become a millionaire, as could Ronald

Steed. I was also dedicated to my men and to the cause that I felt through the company. I was going to accomplish so many good things through my association with this company.

Back in California, I went to work and concentrated on my personal production. I was the top Bellringer with the company the next week following the seminar and would have continued to be the top man if my Cadillac had not had been repossessed by the bank. I had called the bank vice president back in Texas. I had been assured he had given me a chance to get the payment mailed. However, the vice president failed to notify his manager in charge of the repossession order.

Now I was hurt and felt all had been lost. I contacted Bowles and confided in him, as I had done on other occasions. Bowles advised me to let the car go back to the bank, especially when he was told what I was paying for it. David had arranged the payment schedule for me, and because he was in California, the ninety-day contract expired. I had paid an additional $1,100 in order to get a monthly payment contract. However, David secured a high-interest rate on the loan, and I had not taken time to figure it out until the repossession happened.

I took Bowles' advice. He asked me to lease a car instead of trying to get the Cadillac back. I had not received the advance that the company had promised. Bowles rented the car for me to use until arrangements of some kind had been made. I started back to work but was ineffective in my presentations because I was worried about my family having what they needed to live, coupled with the loss of the car.

The California regional meeting was in two days, and Ronald Steed had promised Helen that he would help me when he arrived. I looked forward to talking to Mr. Steed and relating my entire experience surrounding the move to California. I felt David had ill advised me on the company's commitments to my move.

Bowles met Steed at the airport and drove him to the Beverly Hilton Hotel, where the meeting would be held the next day.

I had helped Bowles and the associates plan the meeting agenda. We had invited many well-known guests from Los Angeles to attend the meeting, including the guest speaker, Dr. Robert Schuler from Garden Grove, California.

As they sat in the hotel dining room, Steed told Bowles, "Dwayne, I feel it's time you made a move. You should be building this state by hiring men and also your other states. I want you to name a state manager tomorrow, and I know that you have one man who can do the job if we get him in shape. That man is Richard Martin. What do you think of Richard as a state manager?"

"He is a good man, but he has had a rough time getting started here, and I don't believe he is the man for the job because he is in bad financial shape. He just lost his Cadillac, and besides that, I do not know how he will fair as a colored man in charge of white men. He could not go into the homes of white people with the white associates. He is so sold on you and the company that it sometimes scares me into believing some of the things he says. But his best skill is hiring; he can probably out hire any man with the company."

"You say he lost his car?"

"That's right," Bowles answered. "He probably won't talk to you about it because he is so proud, hardheaded, and independent, and so you may get more out of his wife if you are still planning to get him into shape."

"Okay, I want you to call and have the Martins come over here tonight."

Bowles called, but I was out working and Helen promised him we would be there provided I came back early.

I was driving up in the rental car as Helen hung up the telephone. She relayed the conversation. I had made an appointment on a callback that would produce five contracts within the hour, and I could not miss that appointment, so I told Helen I would talk to Steed early in the morning.

Steed called again as we were talking, and Helen whispered, "It is Mr. Steed."

"I'm not here," I whispered.

"Richard is not here, Mr. Steed."

"Can you come down to this here Beverly Hilton Hotel? I really want to talk to you, and I'll send you back in a cab if you can get here."

"I can get my cousin to babysit and drop me off, so I'll be there in an hour."

She talked me into driving her to the hotel prior to going to my appointment.

"Why does he want to talk to you?" I asked.

"I guess because Dwayne probably told him you wouldn't talk about our problems, and he feels that he should get more information out of me."

I dropped the kids off at her cousin's. If I hurried, I

would make the appointment. I had encouraged Helen to be sure and tell all, leaving nothing out.

Steed was waiting in the lobby when Helen arrived and took her up to his suite. He handed her two hundred dollars before she could say anything and said it was to buy food for the family.

"What do you think your husband is best at with this company?"

"Well, I know he is good in all areas, but because of our problems he has not been able to do the necessary one, place contracts, but he has always wanted to hire men. That's it, hiring men."

"Good, I am relying on your judgment because I know you are probably right, and I will talk to Dwayne tomorrow and get together with him on a hiring job that will pay him two hundred dollars per man. We'll pay off his bills and get his car back. Do you think that will solve his problems?"

"Oh, yes, sir. That's all he needs since he never got the help from the company that David promised. You have helped us tremendously, and this money you gave me will come in handy."

Steed made her think that the decision to give Richard the hiring position was hers. He began to accomplish the scheme he had in the back of his mind by telling her it was God's will that he should help her and that he wanted her to help him.

"I am a man, and I have wanted you since Dallas, and I know that money will cure all your problems. I know it is God's will that you help me tonight. I want you to go to bed with me one time, and I will see to it that you never have to sacrifice again. Remember this, it is not always what you know that will make you rich. It is *who* you know."

He reached for her and she pulled away. He grabbed her again, and she was forced to kiss him. She immediately thought of a way out to have time to think. She had been convinced that Steed would help them, and what would one physical act hurt? She told him that her cousin had to go to work and that she would be at the house with the boys in two hours, and she would be able talk about his request tomorrow.

He told her not to tell anyone, especially Edith. He also told her, "Arrange for Richard to meet with us for breakfast, and then I will leave Richard and Dwayne to plan the meeting and we can have time together."

I had trouble with the rental car and did not make the important appointment, so I picked up the boys and waited at home for Helen. When she arrived and showed me the money that Steed had given and explained what he planned to do for me, I was overwhelmed.

We met Steed and Bowles for breakfast. Steed laid out the plans for Bowles and me to finalize. He asked Helen to come to his room and he would have the hotel send a typewriter up for her to formalize the plans in print so that each one could have a copy. I went to help Dwayne set up the meeting room.

I was outside the meeting room checking on the guest nameplates when Steed came down. Helen had not shown up, but I was not concerned because I knew she was typing. I noticed Steed had lipstick on his lips and teeth but thought he had kissed one of the white associate's wives, not knowing it was Helen who had kissed him. Mrs. Bowles noticed it and told Steed that he had something on his face. Steed stared at me, turned his head, and wiped his mouth. I only smiled in innocence of the truth.

The promotion of state manager was made to one of the older district managers I had hired and trained.

When my promotion was announced as special assistant to the regional manager with the responsibility of hiring, Bowles brought the microphone down into the audience and handed it to me while making the announcement, and the associates cheered.

I stood up and began to acknowledge thanks for the confidence bestowed in me to be the main catalyst in building the State of California. I challenged the managers present to be the cogs in the wheels that carried on with new production and enabled me to move to the other regional states to begin work there.

As I was speaking, Mr. Steed interrupted, saying, "Bring your wife up here, and let me tell you folks, without her, he would be nothing. She is 98 percent of him."

I heard that statement, and it did not sit well with me. My face showed the dismay I felt, and the associates noticed the change in my expression. I had been working hard, and I knew that without me, Helen would be nothing and have nothing, and I showed my first sign of concern.

I had noticed the difference in Helen's attitude and the way she carried herself since the last night after she had returned from the hotel, but I put it aside as being foolish thoughts. I still felt as though Ronald Steed was next to God, especially during the meeting when the movie of Ronald Steed's life was being shown for the edification of the guests.

Helen and Steed left the room when the film started. Steed told the audience that he would give her the honor of selecting the evening dinner menu. I had noticed their leaving but was distracted and thought nothing of their absence.

The meeting ended with Bowles, allowing me to present a motivational speech that went over big.

Dr. Schuler was impressed by my presentation and commented to me after the meeting.

"You are an enlightened individual and an inspired salesman, and I pray that you are strong enough to handle any setbacks that may come to you because of your intense love for the image of this company and the man who heads it."

Coming from such a revered man as Dr. Schuler, I felt like my eyes were suddenly opened. I comprehended the context of what he had stated. I began to see what was happening around me.

Steed sat next to Helen at dinner, and, for the first time, I witnessed him drinking wine, an alcoholic beverage. This was something Steed had never been seen doing before. Dinner was held in the French restaurant at the penthouse level of the Beverly Hilton. The meal and the service were in excellent taste, and many of the participants congratulated Helen on her choice, because, as Steed had reiterated, this was her decision.

After the dinner, I was ready to go home with the assurance that all my problems had been solved, and I could begin to produce and hire on a full-time basis. Helen, who had been aloof toward me throughout most of the day, came up to me as we were preparing to leave. Steed had said good-bye to everyone and had gone to his room.

"Mr. Steed wants me to come by his room to complete typing the agreement."

"What?" I said in a low tone. "I thought you finished that this morning."

"We had trouble getting a typewriter, and then it was time to go to the meeting."

Bill Landry, one of my hires, was close by and overheard the conversation.

"I won't be long. You can come with me if you want to or wait in the lobby, and everyone else will be watching the movie stars come in."

I waited in the lobby, and a TV news camera caught me in the background as they took video of the governor, Ronald Reagan.

I was kidded by Bill Landry about this. Landry was waiting because his wife was intent on watching all the movie stars arrive.

Landry told me that he did not like the way Steed had conducted himself. He did not feel he had projected the image we all knew of him.

"How naive can you be, Richard?" Landry lamented.

I was not following his trend of thought. I had not noticed anything different about Steed. I told Landry that Steed was extra friendly toward Helen and Mrs. Bowles because he knew them better than anyone else.

In the meantime, Steed was in his room with Helen for a second time that day and had given her a one hundred-dollar bill and told her he would send her more money if she could arrange to receive it somewhere so I would not know and not to tell me about the money.

An hour passed and I had become impatient now that I was alone in the lobby. I made a phone call to Steed's room. He told me that Helen was on her way down and that she had waited on a special bottle of wine that he had ordered from room service.

Helen was now in the lobby and paging me.

When I met her, she came up flashing the bottle of wine.

In the meantime, Landry had invited some of the associates to come to his house for socializing, and I had committed to attending.

En route to Landry's, I noticed that Helen had been drinking a lot and her lipstick was fresh, replaced after dinner. I told her I did not approve of the way she had conducted herself all day long and that I was ashamed of her for the second time in our marriage. She was still in a mood foreign to me and did not have much to say during the trip.

Bowles was at Landry's, and I did not expect to see him there. I tried to hide the bottle of wine I was carrying because I remembered what Bowles had set down as a rule for associates in the state.

"There will be no gathering of associates in a party, and they should not be seen drinking in public bars."

Bowles saw the bottle and was the first to say, "Drink it." The Bowles had been drinking while waiting for us to arrive from the hotel.

After the party, we picked up the boys and returned home. I noticed that Helen went immediately to the bathroom and locked the doors. This was something she had not done previously unless there were visitors in the house. Then she went directly to bed without any concern for the boys being tucked in their cots. I followed her this time, and I guess I was suspicious because I tried to have relations with her on purpose and she refused.

I felt that Dr. Schuler and Bill Landry were attempting to open my eyes to what was happening, but to believe that, I would have to suspect Mr. Steed, and that was out of the question. I ruled out as my suspicions as jealousy for Helen's cares for this man whom I admired.

Bowles called a Monday-morning meeting for non-producers but did not make it mandatory. I decided to go but stopped on the way to attend Mass to thank God for all I was going to receive.

The meeting was held at Bowles' home, and on arrival I was met at the door and asked to go into the study. Bowles came in and started in on me by arguing that I should have been on time for the meeting.

"Turn in your kit, Richard," he began. "Obviously you don't appreciate what I have done for you because you show up late for the meeting. I told you that I would never tolerate a man being late for meetings or appointments with me. And tell me this, your wife was not planning to attend Saturday's meeting until Mr. Steed called, was she?"

"Wait a minute. First things first," I rebutted. "As far as my being late for this meeting, I really had not intended to come to it. It was not mandatory and, yes, I am a non-producer, but I am not incapable of producing, and as far as my wife is concerned, she wouldn't have missed that meeting unless she started feeling worse. I don't know what you are angry for. It's as if you know something but you're keeping it to yourself. But let me tell you this, I have a new job to work on. I went to Mass before coming here to thank God for what you and Steed are doing for me."

"Well," continued Bowles, "I didn't know that, but when I called your house, your wife was still in bed and she told me she didn't get up with you and fix you breakfast, so I consider her not to be a good Great National wife. She has to grow up because there have been so many wives who've ruined their husband's careers, and if she doesn't shape up, she'll ruin you."

"Let's lay off her," I stated. "If we had something to fix for breakfast and I wanted it, all I would have to do is ask her. You are going too deep, getting into my personal business. You can have the kit if you really want it, but give me better reasons than what you have told me so far, because nothing you've said has any teeth in it."

Bowles relented and asked me to come in and help with the meeting.

After the meeting, I went home. I confronted Helen after the meeting and told her not to tell Mrs. Bowles anything about our personal affairs because she was telling her husband.

"Like what did he say?" Helen questioned.

I told her everything.

"What he was really saying was that you are no good for me."

She started talking about how she was to blame for not saying the right things. She felt it was her fault but would not tell me why.

She thought Steed had told Bowles about a conquest, yet she felt bad enough to ask to leave the house in order to find a job. I did not stop her. Even though Steed did not want the wives working, I felt it would do her and the family some good.

She needed something to do, and any help would make it easier on us. Helen did not try to find a job that day. Instead, she was with her cousin all day. They went out clubbing with the money Steed had given her and she came home after 2 a.m.

I was angry, and when she walked in, I could tell she had been drinking. I grabbed her, shook her, and wanted for the first time to hit her. I felt that she wanted me to hit her. She had made me feel sorry for her, and I decided to forget about it for the time being.

I began working on interviewing five men a day. I had interviewed fourteen by Thursday, and two had committed to work. I had five tentative and the rest questionable. It had been a good week's work, and I was on schedule with my goal to hire eight men a month.

On Friday morning, I made plans to work on production. My commanders had given me letters of introduction, but Bowles called the house and said he was going out of town. He wanted to turn in the rental car and for me to call the bank and tell them that I would send in the payment so that they could release my Cadillac. I had let Helen use the car to go to a washateria. Bowles wanted me to come over after I made the call to the bank. I told him that she had the car and would be right back. Bowles was disturbed about her using the car. In addition, all I could think was, *Why did he want to turn in the rental car and take me out of production?*

Steed called our home and asked for Mrs. Martin, then he recognized my voice and he nervously asked about a report on recruiting that I had mailed in but he had not received.

Steed was not sure whether I knew anything because, normally, I would have been out of the house and at work by this time of the day.

Steed began to suspect that I might know of his advances toward Helen and decided to call Bowles when his secretary informed him that Bowles was on the other line.

"Dwayne, Steed, look, I want you to terminate Richard Martin and tell me what happens, because I tested his wife and I want to find out whether she betrayed me, and I believe if you terminate him, I'll be able to learn if he knows. Do you have anything on him?"

"Yes, I do, Mr. Steed. He lied to me about the bank payment on his Cadillac, and he was late for a meeting Monday. I could say that he is not doing his job because I told him I would have some letters for him to work on, and he let his wife use the car to go to the washateria rather than come by to pick up the letters and make arrangements to pick up his car. I can especially make something out of the car thing."

"That's a good boy. Go ahead and write him a letter and try to get him out of the house so I can talk to his wife."

Bowles called and asked me to come by to get the letters and talk about the car.

Helen had come back, so I told Bowles I was leaving right away.

When I arrived, to my utter surprise, Bowles presented me with a termination letter outlining the reasons he told Steed he would use.

"I can see that you are intent on terminating me. I guess you don't want to live up to the agreement, or you're jealous that Steed wants to do this for me. You tried it on Monday, and now, after I have had one of the best recruiting weeks since I have been here, you terminate me for reasons that are personal and between you and me. There is not a thing you can point to that is a violation of my contract with the company, even if all that you say is true. But I can see through the way you have purposely misconstrued the real facts, and I am going to accept it until I have time to find out the real reason."

Bowles, realizing that I had no knowledge of Steed's advances, told me, "I am terminating you from this region, but not from the company. If anyone wants to pick you up, they can. I will hold it open and make a final decision tonight."

He realized they could be making a big mistake in terminating me.

In the meantime, company telephone lines were crisscrossing the country with conversation about the termination of Richard Martin.

I had informed Helen, and she was trying to call Steed to find out what was going on. I also tried to call David, but he was not in. We continued to try and contact Steed to no avail.

David called, but I decided not to go the phone because I wanted to wait for Bowles' decision prior to talking to David.

David pressed Helen to try and speak to me. He called Bowles, only to learn that he had terminated me.

"I will pick up Richard and send him to Atlanta, Georgia," David advised Bowles.

Bowles tried to advise him against picking me up until he could find out what Steed wanted to do.

Bowles called me, gave his decision, and advised me to call David. I decided against calling David until 3 a.m. that next morning, when I received a phone call from George Leahy, an associate I had hired.

Leahy informed me, "Richard, Bowles has told us that he terminated you, but he won't tell us why. Man, your neck is on the line and you should be here at the hotel to defend yourself.

"Wait a minute!" I exclaimed. "You mean Bowles told you that he terminated me and you are meeting with him at three in the morning?"

"That's right, man, and we want to find out what's going on. One day you're up and the next day you're out. They are playing games with your life, and since he won't level with us, we don't understand it. Are you coming?"

"No. I don't have transportation."

"Well," replied Leahy. "We'll bring the meeting over there."

Bowles made a mistake and did not use any tact in explaining the termination, because if he had given me the opportunity, he could have handled the situation, but now he had the entire Black group up in arms. George Leahy had pressured Bowles and placed his neck on the line, and he was the wrong person to do that, although he was the most likely. Leahy had an arrest record and was having difficulty obtaining his insurance license. Bowles had promised to help him after he found out why Leahy had been picked up so many times for drunkenness or disturbing the peace. Yet Leahy continued to pressure Bowles into giving them an answer because they all felt that if it happened to me, it could easily happen to them and end their dreams of success. They got nothing out of Bowles, so they asked him to go with them to my house, but he declined.

I was so concerned that I called and woke up David.

"Hello, David. Look, Bowles has terminated me and made a mistake of not handling it tactfully with the Black associates here, and he has them in a meeting right now at this hour. They have called and said they would bring their meeting over here. I wanted to try and get some information on how to handle the situation."

"Yes, I know about the termination. I talked to Bowles today, and he told me why and how he was leaving it hanging for someone else to pick you up. Look, man, I tried to call you today, and I understand you were home but just would not answer the phone. Isn't that right?"

I agreed but told him I was not answering the phone until I had the final decision.

"Look, I was going to send you to Atlanta, but since you didn't have enough faith in me to call, I have changed my mind and you will have to stick it out the best way you can. In addition, you can handle the problem with the men the best way you can because Bowles does not care if they all quit. He'll start over."

I knew that very minute that David was not being truthful and told Helen that he'd lost my friendship.

The men arrived by the time Helen had made coffee and set the table for them. They explained what had transpired with Bowles and wanted to hear my side of the story.

I told them I did not know the real reason but felt that, based on the charges Bowles had made, there was nothing that was in violation of the agent's contract. There was no basis for separation or termination. I explained to them the charges Bowles had made and told them that Bowles had made a rash decision, or perhaps there was something else involved and it may very well have been personal toward me because of the respect everyone gave me instead of Bowles.

I sent the men home because of the late hour, but not before Bill Landry expressed his opinion to the group. Bill was knowledgeable on situations of life. He felt Steed was in some way responsible for all of the sacrifices I had endured, and maybe he was responsible for this termination. Little did we know how right Bill was again.

Bill Landry came by early the next day. I had invited everyone to a barbecue and swim party to get their minds off the calamity. I had convinced them that I would have my job back as soon as I was able to talk to Mr. Steed.

Bill called Bowles' wife, Jackie, who explained that he had left to attend the company meeting in Puerto Rico, but she gave him the phone number in Kansas where Bowles had stopped on his way to Puerto Rico. Bill called him in Kansas and asked what it would take to get me back on the job.

Bowles stated that if I would admit that Bowles was right about everything, he would accept me back. I took the phone from Bill and conceded to Bowles that he was right and that his decision was just. I only wanted to remain with the company long enough to find out why I was terminated. I knew someone was not leveling with me, and I could only imagine who those people might be. I felt that somehow Helen knew something because she had talked to Steed and kept saying that she was responsible for the termination because, as she put it, she was not making breakfast and had used the rental car when she should not have.

The next week was trying for Helen and me. We attempted to talk to Steed in Puerto Rico. We did not have transportation, but George Leahy, because he had confronted Bowles, had his contract cancelled by the company, came by and ran errands every day for us. I worked with Bill Landry for two days, and Leahy still came by to run errands for Helen.

Leahy's wife, Ann, did not have a good relationship with her husband and was looking for some reason to divorce him because of his drinking and smoking pot. She wanted him to quit since he was not making money, and especially because his contract had been cancelled. She had been following him, and she perceived that Leahy was spending time over at my house when it did not seem that I was at home. She came by on a Monday morning and said that her husband did not come home the night before. She told me that she had Leahy followed and wanted the affair between George and Helen to stop.

I was shocked by her statement and immediately tried to convince her that she was wrong. Leahy had been in a wreck the night before and was placed in jail for drunkenness. We knew that because he had called Bill Landry for help. Ann was angry, but I could see that she was serious about her charges. I could not see what

Helen could want in Leahy because he could offer her
no more than I could. Ann was certain that Leahy had
been out with Helen when the accident occurred, but
Helen told me that she had been visiting her cousin. I
tried to explain to Ann where she was wrong but could
not change her convictions. I told her that I would talk
to Helen to definitely prove Ann wrong and call her
that night.

I went to Helen to wake her up and question
her about where she had gone the night before. She
assured me that she had been with her cousin all night.
I remembered that it was her cousin who had called
to report that they had car trouble instead of Helen. I
continued to question Helen. I warned her not to let
any men in the house when I was not there, especially
Leahy. I knew that Helen had gained some respect
from the men when I was the district manager, because
when I was on the road, they called her, and she had
been schooled on how to give them confidence when
they had not struck pay dirt and how to build them up
even more when they had production. I found it easy to
believe her rather than Ann Leahy; however, I was still
concerned that Ann might be right.

That night, Helen's aunt picked her and the boys up
for a visit. I placed a call to Ann Leahy and told her that
I was convinced she was wrong.

Ann stuck to her story. She was convinced that
Helen and her husband were having an affair. She
shocked me again by stating that Helen had called
Leahy. She had listened on an extension phone. She
overheard Helen say she was always lonesome and that
I was not at home enough to sleep with her. I would not

believe that statement either, but Ann added, "What is this talk that your wife has been going around about she and Ronald Steed having an affair at the meeting? Also about him giving her two hundred dollars?"

"I don't know anything about an affair. I would like to know who is saying these things, because if this is really happening, I don't think Helen would be that crazy to talk to anyone about something as explosive as an affair with Mr. Steed."

"You don't know my husband then, because after he gets her high on some pot, she will tell him anything. He told me that she told that story to him, and I have heard it from others as well. You mean you have not heard these stories from the men?"

"No, I haven't heard anything! But I promise you this, I will find out tonight."

I did not know where to turn for help. In a case like this, I would normally talk to Helen, but now I had to talk to her like I had never done before. I knew that if the rumors were wrong, I would hurt her feelings, but if they were true…

As I began to think back to that meeting and the number of times she was in his room, and of the lipstick, I realized that I needed to know the truth.

As soon as Helen arrived home, I had her put the boys to sleep. Then I started to talk to her about all that I had heard about her and Leahy and of the things Ann had told me. I urged her to tell the truth, because if she hedged, I would know.

First, she denied all that I told her but admitted that she did have something she wanted to talk to me about for some time but could not bring herself to hurting me. She was cunning in her explanation, being careful not to admit guilt fully to anything. She told me that nothing had happened; she had done nothing wrong and could not say how the rumors got started because she did not start them. Then she told me that Ronald Steed had tried to kiss her in the elevator.

"He started telling me all kinds of things and asking me questions about Edith and whether I had a miscarriage or hysterectomy in January. Then he started telling me about having all the things I wanted if I would give in to him, and that is when I left. I did not want to tell you because I knew how you felt about him and the company.

"How could a wife tell her husband that Ronald Steed was a womanizer? I did not want to ruin things for you either, but you never talked to me and warned me of what to do when I was approached by men, and if you had, I would have known how to handle it better. I would have been able to tell you before now."

I was incensed by the thoughts going through my mind. Bowles, David, the phone calls, the nervousness of Steed in my presence, his conduct at the meeting, and the convenience of it all and began to tear her story apart. She had stated times and situations that were inconsistent with what I had witnessed. I felt that I could not live with her anymore. I told her that I wanted to get a divorce. I was shifting all the blame to her. I realized that later in life. I did not want to believe anything negative as far as Steed was concerned. But I had to believe. How else could everything have gone so wrong? I knew that I had put him next to God in my life, which weakened me through brainwashing. I had to believe. And then I spoke.

"I always thought that I could love you no matter what you did, and I guarantee you that if I had the money, I would go to Dallas right now and Steed would have to fear for his life.

"In addition, to think that all this time I have felt that I loved and respected this man for the morals he had and for what he was doing for the people and because of his Christian philosophy of life, but now I hate him with a passion for wrecking my life in more ways than one. Bill Landry did not know how close he came to the truth. Now I realize why I was terminated. It was because Steed was afraid you had told me about his conduct.

"There is another reason I knew you were lying, because you said you did not talk to George Leahy or anyone else, but I know that you talked to Bill Landry. I know he called you to tell you how he felt about Steed and how he did not think you conducted yourself properly with Steed at the meeting. I thought Steed was showing favoritism to us because he did not know anyone else better than he did us and the Bowles. I do have enough money to send you home, so tomorrow morning we are going to pack and you will be on your way the next day. You have no choices in this matter, because you did not tell me the truth. Maybe now that I am going to divorce you, you can tell me the truth. No! However, maybe someday you will.

"I want to tell you something right now that I have been keeping from you because I did not want to hurt you. I believe now that if I told you earlier, you probably would have been trying to find another man a long time ago. Do you remember when I was off sick for forty-five days and you thought I had a bladder infection? Well, I did not, and I want you to know that I have been dying for over a year. I have terminal bladder cancer. I took this job to secure your future and the boys' also. Doctor Prince and I have been in constant contact. Those days that you could not find me, I was at the hospital having medical treatments."

Helen stared at me and could see that I was serious, then she moved toward me, but I pushed her back and held her away from me.

"I hope you feel ashamed for what you have done, but I cannot forgive you. I could never forgive you. All I can do is pray that God forgives you and me."

I could not hold her away from me any longer. I embraced her, and tears came to my eyes to match hers.

"What about the children?" she asked.

"I took this job to take care of their future, but because I placed a spiritual trust in Ronald Steed, I have failed, and now I have only one way to turn. God, my parents, and the angels will provide for them. If you have ever prayed, you had better pray now, Helen, because I feel awfully bad about what you have done, even though you will not admit to it. Your silence tells me the truth, even though you will not. I know it is late, but I am going for a midnight walk. I'll be back after I've had time to think things through."

As I walked through the neighborhood streets, I wanted a car to come by and run over me. I was looking for an accident. I sat on the curb and thought about what I had said to Helen. I did not know if my decision was right or not. I began to recite the holy rosary. I knew God had not answered me as I completed the prayers, but I had not changed my mind. I would send them home. I would have to sell my Rolex and the diamond in my tie tack to pay for their tickets.

I arrived back at the house and walked into the bedroom. I tried to convince her that she had something to live for, that I would not divorce her, and that I needed her to take care of the children. She finally realized that she should be thankful that she did not have to go through the agony and pain I had been suffering.

"All of the things you have done are bad in God's eyes. You have a lot to be thankful for, and you need to realize that. Until you do, nothing will be right with you and God. If I were you, I would get on my knees and pray for guidance and forgiveness of my sins. And to show you that I have faith that, through you, my children will grow to be men who walk with God throughout their lives, I'll pray with you."

We prayed together and talked more about them going home to Port Arthur and Welford Street before we were finally able to sleep.

The packing was completed the next evening, and, after a cab ride, Helen and the children boarded the train for Texas. They left not knowing whether they would ever see me alive again. I had the same feeling. It was as if I had died the moment the train pulled out of the station and out of view. I knew my family would take care of Helen and the boys. I called my mother to ask for her help, knowing she would never turn me down, let alone a stranger in need.

I had confided in only one family member since

I knew about the cancer. She was my understanding mother who was suffering and praying for me each day.

I remembered the words Mother spoke.

"God loves you, Richard. You should be thankful that he has warned you as he did for his son, Jesus Christ. You have a chance to prepare yourself for his judgment, so don't fail him. Live

good, pray often, call on our angel, and remember that Daddy and I will pray each day for your health and for your family."

Mother had never failed me, and I knew she would care for Helen and the children.

The Trial

On my way out of the terminal, I ran in to my old friend Brad Morgan. We shook hands and then embraced. We had not seen each other since I had first left Dallas.

Was it irony, or just coincidence, that we met at this tumultuous time in both our lives? Brad had taken a job in California and had come to the station to pick up some goods his wife had shipped to him. He had heard from David that I had been terminated.

"Richard," he said, "if there is anything I can help you with, just let me know. I know the position you're in."

Brad gave me a ride to the apartment building where he was staying temporarily until his family moved to California. He helped me move out of the rental house into a small bachelor's apartment in the same building by paying the start-up fees. We had time to discuss all that had happened to us while we were with the company. I wished that Brad had contacted me after he'd quit. I would have listened to him, and most of what had transpired would not have.

Brad advised me to call John Hooper, who had left the company for similar reasons.

"John is suing Steed, and I know he will be glad to hear from you."

I called John from Brad's telephone. John told me that he wanted to call so many times but had guilt about bringing everyone to the company. He also thought that we would think he was a sorehead.

John and two others were filing suit, charging damages, misrepresentation, violation of contracts, and alienation of affection for one who had lost his wife. The main pretext that brought everyone to the company, the immoral conduct of the president, which was the opposite that everyone thought and were told when they were introduced to Steed and Great National, helped the cases. They felt they had good cases, but no one had been hurt more than I.

I called my friend Ronald DeWitt, the builder, who was shocked to find out about me leaving the company. He had been told by David and others that I was making lots of money in California and to stop offering me jobs.

DeWitt arranged for air passage to Dallas and offered me a position with his company. I took advantage of the offer with first thoughts of getting to Dallas in order to hurt Steed.

On the plane ride back to Dallas, the flight attendant dropped a Bible in my lap by accident. Apologizing, she tried to retrieve it, but I told her I would read it unless someone had asked for it specifically. She shook her head no.

The Bible had fallen open to a verse in Job. I began interpreting the words and got the message from God's words about how I would complete his mission to help my family. As I read the story of Job, I saw how the characters in my life resembled the people in the Bible verses. I could almost hear God talking to me out loud.

> *"Richard, if someone attempts a word with you, will you mind? For how can you refrain from speaking out against this man who has wrecked your life? Behold, you have instructed many, and have made firm their feeble hands. Your words have upheld the stumbler; you have strengthened his faltering knees. You canst not believe the things you have heard about this Lion; but now it comes to you. You are impatient. It touches your self, and you are dismayed. Is not your piety a source of confidence and your integrity of life your hope? Reflect now on what has happened. What innocent person perishes? You! And since when are uprights like you destroyed?*
>
> *"As I see it, those who plow for mischief and sow trouble shall reap the same. By the breath of God Almighty, you can be assured that they will perish, though that man roars now, though the king of the beasts cries out, have I not broken the teeth that tied you to him? The old man perishes for lack of prey, and the upright of the land are no longer close. Can you as a man be righteous as against God? Can a mortal be blameless against his Maker? They unlike you die without knowing wisdom that is yours now!"*

(Job 1-42, NIV)

I realized that it was no quirk of fate that this Bible had fallen into my lap and to a page open to the text that explained my life with Great National as if I were the main character in that verse. Now I knew I must fulfill the final part of that message; I must be the catalyst to bring to an end this man's dynasty. I could not wait for John Hooper or anyone else. This was my answer. God had selected me to come home early, but before that, my mission had to be completed. It was plain and clear that I needed to help in the ruination of the tyrant who had used God as his vehicle to plow for mischief, fortune, and lust.

DeWitt picked me up at the airport, and I explained what had happened from beginning to the end. I told him about being enlightened about the mission that I felt I needed to accomplish while I was high in the heavens aboard the aircraft. Then I told DeWitt why I did not have time on my side.

DeWitt joined me in my mission. He contacted his brother-in-law, George Washington, who was one of the most respected attorneys in the Texas legislature. I had met Washington that last December, when I sold him a contract in San Antonio, where he was also the county museum curator. After visiting with me, Washington jumped at the opportunity to represent me. A case of such magnitude would propel him politically and add credence to his bills to reform the insurance companies in the state. Washington prepared a suit for $2 million in damages on my behalf and prepared a class action lawsuit for thirty million in damages for all the associates hired by the company in 1968 and 1969. After receiving completed questionnaires from the associates, charges were filed against Steed and the company.

The company's operation was halted by the insurance commissioners in all states based on the filing. The case was brought to trial one month after being filed. With encouragement from Mr. Washington, the case was strengthened by the support of the state insurance commissioner. There had been serious investigations into Great National by the commissioner's office for two years prior.

Mr. Washington was able to get the support of Helen and twenty-three other material witnesses who were former employees or associates' wives. This, coupled with the showing of the Ronald Steed story, the movie that purported all of the good about the man and was used primarily to recruit associates and secure investors, proved to be sufficient enough evidence to secure a guilty verdict and award damages to me in the individual suit and to the other associates in the class action suit.

Steed refused to testify during the trial. He had flown to Florida on a prearranged trip with his secretary, with whom he had been having an affair the entire time she worked for the company.

He had also prearranged what was thought to be a miracle youth restorer. There had been two cases where men had received transfusions of sheep's blood. Steed believed his medical advisor and had flown to Florida to be the third recipient of this miraculous transfusion. His body rejected the sheep's blood, and he died the following day.

Learning of his flight to avoid prosecution on the criminal charges that had come out in the trial, and of his subsequent unusual death, the court subpoenaed his secretary, who revealed all of the diaries she kept and all of the details relevant to hiring and control of agents utilized by Steed.

The final court date had come full circle. It was exactly two years since I had first learned about Great National, Ronald Steed, and my illness. I had been the instrument necessary to crush the enemies of honest people and of the associates who were sure to follow if this man had not been stopped. My health had deteriorated, and I had frequent visits to my friend and doctor in Dallas.

The scene at the courthouse created pandemonium as reporters tried to question me and Congressman Washington. With both parts of the case being awarded to the plaintiffs, we knew there would be appeals. Prospects for monetary awards were not guaranteed, and the other attorneys, including Mr. Washington, felt a notice of the company's bankruptcy filing would surely follow.

Helen made her way to where I was standing.

"The boys are outside in the car. They need you, until…until…"

Her voice cracked, and her tearful face showed the wear and tear of many sleepless nights since I had sent her back home. I cut her off.

"I forgive you, Helen. God forgives you. You were a part of my mission, and what you did had to be done. You must forget about the past and focus on your future and that of the boys. I know you can do it now, and God will be at your side. I will be there to remind him. Now let's go take those boys to see their grandparents."

The Healing

The drive to Port Arthur seemed to pass by too fast. There had been long conversations with my doctor and friend about the Great National experience. He was driving me to the family celebration. However, there had also been a lot of crying, praying for healing, and forgiveness.

While Dr. Prince drove, I opened my Bible and reflected on the scripture in Psalms

> Blessed is he who has regard for the weak; the Lord delivers him in times of trouble. The Lord will protect him and preserve his life; he will bless him in the land and not surrender him to the desire of his foes. The Lord will sustain him on his sickbed and restore him from his bed of illness.
>
> I said. 'O Lord, have mercy on me. Heal me, for I have sinned against you,'
>
> My enemies say of me in malice,

'When will he die and his name perish?'

Whenever one comes to see me, he speaks falsely, while his heart gathers slander. Then he goes out and spreads it abroad.

All of my enemies whisper together against me; they imagine the worst for me, saying,

'A vile disease has beset him; he will never get up from the place where he lies.'

Even my close friend, whom I trusted; he who shared my bread has lifted up his heel against me.

But you, O Lord, have mercy on me. Raise me up, that I might repay them. I know that you are pleased with me, for my enemy does not triumph over me. In my integrity, you uphold me and set me in your presence forever."

Psalms 41:1-12, NIV

When we arrived at 1136 Welford, there were many family members, neighbors, and friends waiting to welcome me home.

Some of the friends I did not recognize. It is amazing how one forgets names but remembers faces when they go back home after being away for years. They had all kept up with the trial. They knew of my condition and wanted to pray for me and congratulate me at the same time.

There was a big feast. Uncle Merrill and Aunt Ernestine from Sabine, Texas, had brought freshly cooked pork and seafood from Grangers in Sabine Pass. My dad, Moses, had roasted a turkey, and Mother had made large vats of crab gumbo. Mr. Joe from 1108 had brought pies he baked at Mrs. Barnes' Cafeteria. Other family and friends had brought their own specialties.

Over eighty people attended. The backyard was packed and flowed over into the two adjoining yards. I noticed every time that I was near this mulatto-looking relative that I would feel full of life. At least I assumed he was a relative from Louisiana. After all, he had been hanging with my uncle Oris from Lafayette most of the time. I moved close to this man and felt a chilling feeling go through my body. I reached for the man's right hand. In his left hand was a glass of lemonade, and he held two of Miss Prova's teacakes with his fingers. He sat those down on a nearby picnic table and placed his left hand on my shoulder. Then he touched my chest and then my stomach. I saw all this, and it appeared that Uncle Oris and others around us did not.

"What's your name, cousin? I don't remember you," I said.

"You mean to say you don't remember me? Just think for a minute and it will come to you," the stranger offered.

"Are you from Grandma Rose's side of the family?" I asked.

"Why don't you go and ask your father who I am. He knows me."

Seeing my father, Moses, busy serving up meats, I responded. "Okay, I'll do that. You just wait here till I come back."

I walked over to where Daddy was, and along the way I gave a few hugs and back pats to family members and friends. Some of the women remarked, "You look fabulous," and, "Boy, you look good."

"I feel great," I remember saying.

As I approached, Daddy stared at me and dropped the knife in his right hand and the plate of meat in his left hand. He looked at me like there was something very different about the way I looked. I bent down to get the knife, and Daddy went for the plate of spilled meat. While on our knees, Daddy asked,

"What is it that's so different about you? Why do you look so much better than when you came here four hours ago?"

"I don't know, Daddy. Even some of the women said I look different. The truth is, I feel great. Maybe it's because of the party and all you guys are doing to make me feel at home. But Daddy, I need to know, who is that light-skinned man standing by Uncle Oris?"

Daddy looked in Oris' direction. "Which man? I only see your uncle Alfonse." He was daddy's oldest brother. I looked in that direction, and the man was not there. I ran over to Uncle Oris and Uncle Alfonse. Everyone noticed that I had moved much faster than the slow crawl I possessed on arrival.

"Is this the Richard who came here dragging his body around?" asked Uncle Oris. "You would never know he has cancer."

"Uncle Oris, where is the light-skinned man that was here with you a few minutes ago?" I asked.

"I'm sorry, Shah,"

Uncle Oris said, using the familiar Creole term to address a family member.

"I don't remember no light-skinned man next to me. Come to think, as I look around, I don't see no light-skinned men here."

"But he has been with you most of the day. Surely you talked to him. It looked like he was talking to you."

I moved quickly through the backyards. Not finding the stranger, I looked in the house and then out front where people were in groups, talking and laughing.

"Any of you see a light-skinned man with long hair come this way?" I shouted.

"Not me."

"I didn't."

"Not since I've been here. We haven't left this tub of beer for three hours."

I walked back into the house and sat down in Mother's bedroom. Mother walked in.

"Your daddy said you look different and was looking for a man, but nobody remembers him. Are you all right? How do you feel? I mean, you look great!"

"Mother, I know he was here. He touched me. He touched my chest and my stomach."

Crying, she bent over to where I sat, hugged me tightly, and whispered, "You should have your doctor friend check you out tomorrow."

Doctor Prince had not left for Dallas and was still at the party. I convinced him to stay over and accompany me to St. Mary's Hospital to run some tests again. Dr. Prince noticed the changes and needed to know why the recent jaundice look in my skin had cleared up and why I had so much more strength. He was overwhelmed when he shook my hand with that big Texas grip that he remembered from years past.

The tests and PET scans were completed in the morning on the next day, and I sat waiting in the recovery room of the outpatient clinic for the results.

Doctor Prince skipped into the room and was all smiles as he sat down and placed his arm around me.

"No signs of cancer. There is no cancer. All your test levels are like those of a healthy teenager. This is unbelievable. Last week we saw test results that said you were terminal. I don't know what happened. I had them run and re-run the tests. I don't know. I don't know what could have happened!" he continued to rant.

I did not speak. My thoughts went back to how I felt whenever I was near the stranger. And then he touched me all over. And I felt good; I felt great! And then I could not find him. It was like only I could see him.

I grabbed my friend's arm and led him into the hospital chapel. "Come pray with me awhile. I need to give thanks for an answer to the prayers of many."

We knelt at the altar railing.

"Bob, just let me read the letter I wrote to be read at my death.

"'To my mother, my wife, my sons, my family, and my friends, I will be called to rest with the Lord in just a little while. God called me because it was necessary. He gave me a mission to accomplish in order that I might save my soul and have my prayers answered. We have all done our part, and soon he will take me from you, but do not be saddened for me. My life has been full, and you have helped me to live it. Give praise, instead, to the Lord God Almighty, that he will allow you to join me.

"I feel that I can truly relate to the life of our Savior, Jesus Christ. He lived, taught, was tempted, was scourged, given passion, was crucified, and died. I have lived, taught, been tempted, and made to sacrifice, suffered, and I died. He lived the perfect life. Mine has been imperfect. The Lord forgave those who surrounded Jesus for their inequities, and I forgive those of you who hurt me as I lived.

"My final wish is that you forgive each other. Do not hold grudges against my mother, my wife, my sons, my family, or my friends. You are all a part of my life that will be read in the mighty heavens. What wrong you have done toward me, God forgives you. He planned it that way, and my sufferings came not from you but from the great test of God Almighty. Keep peace within your hearts, and I will remind the Lord often to give you his blessings. I loved you one and all.'

"Bob, I made peace with God and with all my loved ones, especially Helen. I forgave her completely. And now I am healed. I believe my mother is right when she says that I was touched by our angel or if it is one of God's miracles."

I paused, then said,

"I'll be ready to leave after I rest and pray here for about an hour."

Doctor Prince left me and closed the doors to the chapel on his way out.

The good news spread all over the west side that day.

A month passed. In Port Arthur, I was tiring of all the congratulations and people wanting to touch and pray with me. Knowing that my health was good, I contacted Brad Morgan, who was working for Atlantic Richfield. Brad told me the oil companies were hiring marketers. I went back to California and interviewed with Mobil Oil and Humble Oil Company for a sales representative position. I was hired the same day I interviewed with Humble.

The credentials I had achieved and the skills I possessed created a good fit for Humble.

My family joined me, and we lived in Los Angeles. When Pamela, our only daughter, was born, we moved to Carson, California. It was about that time that Rody, my eldest sister, and her three children moved from Texas to Carson following her marriage to Warren Maryland. Rody and I enjoyed having family close and shared many good times together.

In 1974, I bought a house in Granada Hills, California, to be closer to my territory with Exxon Company, which had changed its name from Humble. It was there that all the problems in my marriage started to manifest themselves. Because of the kids, Helen and I kept making it work.

There would never be a settlement from the Great National lawsuit. Great National went into bankruptcy and receivership. Later, it was bought by another company.

Then the finances started to tighten, and the only way out was to sell the house and move. Adding a swimming pool and those additional expenses could not be budgeted, coupled with too much partying and nightlife for both of us. We moved to a house in Harbor City, California. It was there that we knew divorce was inevitable. Helen told me she had filed for welfare. I found out that she had lied about me not living in the house. I could not convince her to cancel the government handout. I moved out into an apartment until I could convince her to stop the welfare.

I moved back home with the children about a month

later. I prayed that I could make every attempt to make the marriage work even to the point of buying a new Cadillac that Helen loved dearly, so much so that she rode in it all the time. The car was the catalyst that made divorce the only option.

Labor Day week was approaching, and I planned to take the children on vacation to Texas. Arriving at home from work, I learned that Helen had come to the house and taken the Cadillac. It would take me into the world of private investigating in order to find out where she lived to get the car back for our Texas trip. Searching through her notes and checking the phone bills, I was able to match phone numbers with an address. I talked to Helen's cousin, whom she confided in, and reluctantly gave me a lead. It led me to an apartment in Fox Hills, but her friend had just moved. I had friends at the post office and was able to secure the forwarding address. Driving by her friend's house that night, I saw the Cadillac in an open garage. Making a scene by taking the car was not the right thing to do, so I called the LAPD, who met me at the site. I explained to the police officers that the car was registered in my name and she had taken it without my permission.

The police officers went to the house and confronted the man and Helen, and, upon checking the registration in the glove box, they told her that they would allow me to take my car. I picked up a fellow worker, drove back to the area, and had my friend drive my company car back to my house. My friend Danny convinced me that I should sell the car because it would continue to cause riffs in the relationship. After taking the children to Texas in the Cadillac, we returned to California. One week after returning from vacation, I arranged a date with a young woman from the Exxon office, whom I had been introduced to over nine months prior with the Los Angeles and Orange districts combined. I picked her up in the Cadillac. She was impressed, but I told her that it meant nothing to me and it would be sold soon. I sold the car one week later after placing an advertisement in the *Times*.

That date was with Catherine and would lead from a great friendship and relationship to marriage after my divorce from Helen. I won custody of the children and had to draw on the skills that Moses and Ida had taught me. I had to perform all the household chores, comb Pam's hair, and dress her and the boys. I had no problem in coordinating school, lunches, dinner, homework, and spending time with the children. I still had to wash clothes and complete the yard work. And let us not forget my coaching duties for the boys' little league baseball teams. My only relaxation came with Friday night bowling. I had become an excellent bowler. I had rolled numerous three hundred games and seven hundred and eight hundred series. While bowling in a league at Gable House in Torrance, I established the longest average of seven hundred series ever recorded at Gable House for eight consecutive weeks. I started bowling on weekends in tournaments. Pam would always tag along with me. When I would win a tourney and over five hundred dollars, and that was often, Pam would have to be in the pictures taken of the champion. Therefore, she made the *Bowling News* along with her dad. In December of 1979, I won my first big tourney. It was a winner-take-all eliminator. I took home one thousand dollars. I had promised my sister Rody that if I won, I would share it with her. Rody had been a life-saver for watching the children when I had a company meeting or when I was in a tourney. I surprised Rody with three hundred dollars.

I had been dating Catherine and was able to give her a Christmas gift from the winnings. She talked of getting herself a new overcoat. My gift was two hundred Susan B. Anthonys. The rest I spent on the children's Christmas. For the next year, I would win a tourney at least twice a month.

I came to understand that my prayers were being answered and felt that when I bowled it was a divine guidance, perhaps another angel, who caused me to concentrate and bowl those perfect games and gain tournament victories.

The Reunion

In August of 1980, Ida's family, the Mitchells, held a family reunion. All the children scattered from California to Colorado to Virginia came home for the reunion. Moses retired from Gulf, and they attended Mass every morning, when good health allowed them.

Ida attended revivals and charismatic meetings of ecumenical beliefs. She was moved to accept Jesus Christ as her Savior and become a born-again Christian. She continued to practice her Christianity in the Catholic Church.

All Moses and Ida's children arrived for the celebration. The neighborhood had changed. The house and rear apartments at 1112, where they were visited by the stranger, was no longer there. A mysterious fire damaged it in 1974. Moses purchased it for an unbelievable price. He demolished the house and made a side yard for his garden.

The old family house had been remodeled. The Martin family was in the living and dining rooms, talking about old times. As stories of the past were told, many talked about how, as children, the Martins never wanted for food, shelter, clothing, or love. Even with eight children, there always seemed to be enough of everything to go around. There were remarks about how blessed this Martin family had been.

Carl, the seventh born, an associate Baptist preacher in Dallas, led the family in prayer, and everyone held hands in a sort of circle. Children and grandchildren were together.

"Let us bow our heads in prayer. Dear Lord and ever-bountiful Jesus, we give thanks today for this homecoming. We are indeed thankful for our safe arrivals, and we ask your blessings on family members who cannot be with us. We ask, most of all, Lord, for your continuing blessings on our parents, Moses and Ida, who through the years have done their best to raise us in a spiritual way and cause us to remember from where our blessings have come.

"Lord, you gave us, their children, the best of parents. Their sacrifices through the years to ensure that we got the right guidance to cause us to be more like them in our family lives is a sacrifice we shall never forget. Lord, we come to you in prayer like strangers that the distances between where we now live have caused. We pray that this reunion brings us close again. Indeed, Lord, you have taken a special liking to this family and have had your angels watching over us all. Surely angels have been here, for you said in Hebrews 13:1-2, 'Keep on loving each other as brothers. Do not forget to entertain strangers, for some people have entertained angels without knowing it.' We thank you, Lord."

Touched by Carl's prayer, many wept. Ida broke from the circle and sat on the couch.

"Everyone, please take a seat. There is a story I must tell you."

Family members took seats and sat on the floor around her.

"Carl, your prayer is the answer to a question your father and I have had unanswered for many years. We have wanted to know how we were able to feed and clothe you all during so many hard times, the refinery strikes, damaging hurricanes, floods, and so many other problems that we faced financially, but you have given us our answer, and we are so proud of the successes that our children have had in life and with their own families.

"While it is very important to entertain angels, it is even more important to know what sort of angels we are entertaining, lest you entertain the wrong kind unawares!

Think of Richard's return to health. He will tell you of the stranger he encountered in his life. It reminds me of the words of a prayer that I taught you all.

'Angel of God, my Guardian Dear, to whom God's love commits me here. Ever this day be at my side, to light and guard and rule and guide.'

You see, we were never afraid to entertain strangers, and we now believe that we entertained the right angel many times but were unaware until today. It always took a visit back to Welford Street for my children to be touched and on their return to their homes, here and in other states, to excel in their endeavors and find relief in their health. Those two china plates hanging on the wall," she said as she pointed to them,

"are the only two left from a china set on which we always served food from the time we were married until my children broke most of them. I am not sure if either of these was the one touched by a special person, but I continue believing they are. Moses and I have never told this *entire* story to anyone. It started over forty-two years ago. In those days, Moses rode home for lunch on a Gulf Oil refinery horse. Vincent was our only child, and I was expecting with Rody.

"And on this summer day…"

Afterword

CONTRIBUTED BY CARL BERTRAM MARTIN

This is a remarkable story of a stranger. I can remember, I was the age of seven, and my mother had me on her lap and my brother Anthony by her side on our daybed. She was relating in detail the story of a man she and my father had held in reverence by feeding him. The story began as she talked about a tall white man one summer day in 1938; our elder brother, Vincent, was only ten months old at that time.

From the beginning of this true story and the historical facts of this miracle that are ongoing at this present time, the whole family has been and still is being blessed, all eight of us. The words of that man, who we all know is an angel of the Lord, our God, are still heard. It is our belief, even to this day and forevermore, that our parents did entertain an angel unawares, and that truth still rings in our entire family.

So let us deal with the facts of this story. The angel said to my mother and father after they had fed him: "From this day forward your family will not ever be without food or shelter."

As a young child, I had a very inquiring mind. I kept asking my mother and daddy, "What did this angel mean by what he said?" and, as always, the same answer was, "We will always have food to eat and a house to live in forever." However, this was not enough for me, so as the years went by, the Word of God, the Bible, became food for my spirit, and the Word gave me the answer I needed. In Psalm 37:25, it reads, "I was young and now I am old, yet I have never seen the righteous forsaken or their children begging bread."

The second part of the message from the messenger (the angel) was shelter. The meaning is this: When we pray or cry unto the Lord like David did in the book of Psalms: "Hear my cry, O God: listen to my prayers. From the ends of the earth I call to you. I call as my heart grows faint; lead me to the rock that is higher than I. For you have been our refuge, a strong tower against the foe" (Psalm 61:1-3).

Moses and Ida Martin had the good fruit of generosity.

The poor people are often the most generous. They know what it is like to be in need. They willingly share what they have. How often do we think about it, sharing with unwavering faith, giving to others at a point of our own need? Without a second thought, our father and mother provided food to families on the west and east sides of Port Arthur, Texas. *Oh, what a legacy to live up to.*

In our own way and in our own little worlds, I believe we have. The legacy now is in us and our children.

God wants us to trust him so that we can be free to give like our parents did, or "like the widow who gave Elijah her last meal" (1 Kings 17:12). God wants us to respond to others with compassion and generosity.

I believe that Moses and Ida were always teaching, sometimes without knowing the theological virtues or one of the three spiritual graces, faith, hope, and charity, drawing the soul of man to God according to a word of faith, hope, and charity. My parents, by the world's standard, had the right to only think of themselves but chose not to look away from needs of others.

Moses and Ida's firstborn child had a disfigured right hand. Vincent overcame many obstacles in his life and victoriously lived for sixty-two years. At the age of forty-one, our mother was with child once again. Our parents needed a challenge to utilize the time and gifts they had available to share because the older children were now on their own. A baby girl was to be the eighth child born in our family. I was only nine years old at that time and was set in my ways. I was the baby for nine long years. Reader, you can draw your own conclusion about this fact; however, I will give you mine. I was upset to say the least. I was no longer upset after our mother and our new baby sister were home from St. Mary's Hospital. She was the best-looking baby I had ever seen. At the age of eight, Althea Marie Martin began to resist the love of our parents. We could all see her rebellion to authority. Our sister could find fault in just about everything. It would only be through the love of our mother and intercession by our angel that one day in the future she would find God and change her life.

In spite of all problems we as a family had and are having today, that angel of the Lord is always with us to keep destiny clear, to share with our neighbor, and keep hope alive.

Our mother and father did not have a lot of money, but what they did have was a lot of love. It is love that does not look away.

Most of my brothers and sisters have had the responsibility to respond to people such as these. If we believe in the commands of the Bible, the example of our Lord, and the Welford Street angel, then our answer must be yes and amen.

Bibliography

History of Port Arthur: taken in part from Handbook of Texas online: Port Arthur http://www.tshaonline.org/handbook/online/articles/PP/hdp5.html (10/3/2007)

Keith L. Bryant, Jr., *Arthur E. Stilwell: Promoter with a Hunch* (Nashville: Vanderbilt University Press, 1971).

Joseph L. Clark, *Texas Gulf Coast: Its History and Development* (4 vols., New York: Lewis Historical Publishing, 1955).

William Ford Stewart, *Collision of Giants: The Port Arthur Story* (San Antonio: Naylor, 1966). WPA Federal Writers' Project, *Port Arthur* (Houston: Anson Jones, 1939).

John W. Storey (author, "*The Origins and Formative Years of Lamar University, 1921-1942*")

History of the Prince Hall Masons

(http://northbysouth.kenyon.edu/2000/Fraternal/
mason-princy%20P..htm)